Prayers that Bring Healing

John Eckhardt

CHARISMA
HOUSE

Most CHARISMA HOUSE BOOK GROUP products are available at special quantity discounts for bulk purchase for sales promotions, premiums, fund-raising, and educational needs. For details, write Charisma House Book Group, 600 Rinehart Road, Lake Mary, Florida 32746, or telephone (407) 333-0600.

PRAYERS THAT BRING HEALING by John Eckhardt
Published by Charisma House
Charisma Media/Charisma House Book Group
600 Rinehart Road
Lake Mary, Florida 32746
www.charismahouse.com

Unless otherwise noted, all Scripture quotations are from the New King James Version of the Bible. Copyright © 1979, 1980, 1982 by Thomas Nelson, Inc., publishers. Used by permission.

Scripture quotations marked CEV are from the Contemporary English Version, copyright © 1995 by the American Bible Society. Used by permission.

Scripture quotations marked KJV are from the King James Version of the Bible.

Scripture quotations marked THE MESSAGE are from *The Message: The Bible in Contemporary English*, copyright © 1993, 1994, 1995, 1996, 2000, 2001, 2002. Used by permission of NavPress Publishing Group.

Scripture quotations marked NIV are from the Holy Bible, New International Version. Copyright © 1973, 1978, 1984, International Bible Society. Used by permission.

Scripture quotations marked NLT are from the Holy Bible, New Living Translation, copyright © 1996. Used by permission of Tyndale House Publishers, Inc., Wheaton, IL 60189. All rights reserved.

Cover design by Bill Johnson

Library of Congress Cataloging-in-Publication Data
Eckhardt, John, 1957-
  Prayers that bring healing / by John Eckhardt. -- 1st ed.
      p. cm.
  ISBN 978-1-61638-004-5
  1. Spiritual healing--Christianity. 2. Spiritual healing--Biblical
teaching. I. Title.
  BT732.5.E29 2010
  234'.131--dc22

                              2010005216

E-book ISBN: 978-1-61638-249-0

15 16 17 18 19 — 13 12 11 10 9
Printed in the United States of America

CONTENTS

INTRODUCTION

EXPECT to BE HEALED

And, behold, a woman, which was diseased with an issue of blood twelve years, came behind him, and touched the hem of his garment.

—Matthew 9:20, KJV

RECENTLY, THE LORD has impressed me to share with God's people the importance of putting a demand on the anointing. The word *demand* means "a seeking or state of being sought after." It means pressing forward despite obstacles to get to a place where the anointing is and expecting it to fall on you. The woman with the issue of blood put a demand on the healing anointing and received her miracle. She expected that once she pushed through that crowd, pushed past the disappointment of years of failed treatments, and pushed against the stigma of being unclean, she would be healed.

Too often God's people do not receive miracles and healing because they do not place a demand on the anointing. They don't push forward because they don't expect that something miraculous will happen.

Sometimes believers let themselves get discouraged. Let me tell you this: Don't let the devil talk you out of your healing.

1

Put your mind on God. You have to press through discouragement and frustration so that you don't miss your miracle. Don't let anyone stop you. You have to press through—press through traffic, press through the parking lot, press through people coming in the door—but don't get upset. Just stay in the Spirit and get to the place where the anointing is and reach up and get your miracle. Just like the woman who pressed, reached, and was healed by touching Jesus's garment, you too can press, reach up, and grab your healing.

God's Healing Is Available to All!

Healing is available to *all* during the kingdom age. It is amazing that some Christians still believe that God puts sickness on His people. Some may ask, "God, why do You allow this sickness to come upon my body?" They feel, or may have been told by a church leader, that it is the will of God for them to suffer sickness and not be healed. However, that is not biblical. God does not put sickness on *His* people. Jesus died so that we might be healed. I do believe that there may be times when God allows sickness, especially for rebellion or disobedience. But for God's people, we can expect to live in health and to be healed of all our diseases because of what Jesus did on the cross.

When Jesus came, He announced the coming of the kingdom of God. In the kingdom of God, where His presence and glory dwell, no sin or sickness can coexist. We are in the kingdom of God now, but it is not fully manifested. However, it can be established in your life and in your heart. Wherever Jesus preached the message of the kingdom, He healed people. Healing accompanies the kingdom message. This is the kingdom age where you don't have to be sick, broke, or run over by the devil. That is GOOD NEWS! You don't have to be sick, broke, poor, or confused any longer. Sickness and disease are works of the devil, and Jesus came and "disarmed principalities and powers, He made a public spectacle of them, triumphing over them" (Col. 2:15).

Healing comes with the territory. When you are in Christ, you can expect to be healed. Mark 16:17–18 says, "And these signs will follow those who believe: In My name they will cast out demons; they will speak with new tongues; they will take up serpents; and if they drink anything deadly, it will by no means hurt them; they will lay hands on the sick, and they will recover." So not only should you expect to be healed, but you should also know that you are to pass that healing on to all those around you. That is true kingdom living.

JESUS HEALS ALL MANNER OF SICKNESS

Sickness and disease are the worst things that can happen to an individual. Jesus cares about people. He cares about the things that make the abundant life He paid for miserable and unbearable. That is why He had no problem breaking man-made religious laws and stale traditions to see to it that people were healed. He had great compassion on the people who came to Him to be healed. In Matthew 9:36, the Bible says that "when [Jesus] saw the multitudes, He was moved with compassion for them, because they were weary and scattered, like sheep having no shepherd." Jesus cares very deeply that you are hurting and suffering. He doesn't want that for you. That is why He made a way for every sickness, ailment, illness, dysfunction, and disease to be healed and for you to be made whole.

When Jesus walked the earth, there was nothing that Jesus didn't heal. When He left, He sent the Holy Spirit, who works in us to have the full extent of salvation that Jesus paid for on the cross. So just know that what was good for the people then is good for us now, because Jesus is the same yesterday, today, and forever (Heb. 13:8). God does not change (Mal. 3:6). There is no shadow of turning with Him (James 1:17). Because of God's faithfulness we can trust that if He healed then, He will heal today.

Matthew 4:23 says, "Jesus went about all Galilee, teaching in their synagogues, preaching the gospel of the kingdom, and healing *all kinds of sickness* and *all kinds of disease* among the people" (emphasis added). Jesus healed every disease or sickness people came to Him with—no exceptions. There was nothing too hard for Him. So don't let the devil or the doctor tell you that you have something that's incurable. It might be incurable to the doctor, but it's not incurable to Jesus Christ.

> When evening had come, they brought to Him many who were demon-possessed. And He cast out the spirits with a word, and healed all who were sick.
>
> —Matthew 8:16

From the verse above, it doesn't appear that Jesus told people it wasn't the will of God for them to be healed or that God wanted them to suffer. He never said, "God wants you to carry this for a while to teach you something."

The prophet Isaiah says that Jesus bore our griefs and sorrows (Isa. 53:4). In Matthew 8:17, it says He took our infirmities and sickness. What causes so much grief and so much sorrow? Sickness and disease. When you're not healthy, you can't enjoy the blessings and the fullness of God.

Isaiah 53 is the redemptive chapter. Verse 5 talks about being healed by the stripes of Jesus. The Bible says that Jesus took thirty-nine lashes on His back and body. There are thirty-nine major categories of sickness and disease. Every stripe that Jesus endured took care of a different sickness and disease.

Young's Literal Translation puts Isaiah 53:4 this way: "Surely our sicknesses he hath borne, and our pains—he hath carried them." God doesn't even want people to be in pain. Millions of dollars are spent on pain relief. Toothaches, headaches, neck pain, earaches, joint pain, back pain—Jesus delivers you from pain. Pain is not the will of God for you. Jesus died so you could be healed from both sickness *and* pain.

HOW YOU CAN BE HEALED

God has a lot of ways to heal us based on the redemptive work of Christ. It is something Jesus paid for—something He suffered for. His desire for you to be healed and walk in divine health is the reason He went through so much pain and suffering. He was taking upon Himself the pain and suffering of humanity. Therefore, He has made healing available to you through many avenues. They are:

1. Healing through the laying on of hands (Luke 4:40)

He didn't tell them it wasn't God's will for them to be healed. Everyone who came to Jesus got healed. No exceptions.

2. Healing through deliverance (Matt 8:16)

Demons can be the reason why people are sick in their bodies. They may have a spirit of infirmity. See also Luke 8:2.

3. Healing through breaking curses (Gal. 3:13)

People are plagued with generational demons of infirmity such as diabetes, high blood pressure, certain heart conditions, and more. If there is a generational curse that is activating sickness in your body, know that because Jesus was made a curse for us, you can tell the devil that he will not put this sickness in your body. Tell him, "I don't care if my mother, grandmother, or great-grandmother had this disease; the curse stops here. I break it in the name of Jesus." Begin to rise up and use your authority! Say, "I am not cursed. I am blessed. My body is blessed with healing, in Jesus's name."

4. Healing through anointing oil (Mark 6:13)

Anointing oil represents the Spirit of God and the anointing. The anointing is what drives sickness and disease out of our bodies. The anointing oil breaks yokes of bondage (Isa. 10:27), and sickness is a form of bondage.

5. Healing through faith (Mark 11:23)

For some people, sickness is a mountain. It's always in their way. It seems like something they can't overcome. But Mark

11:23 says that when you have faith and don't doubt, you will speak to a mountain and it will move. So speak to that mountain of sickness; don't climb it! You have to talk to mountains: "Lupus, be removed and cast in the sea!" "Cancer, be removed and cast in the sea!" But don't doubt in your heart. This is why you have to be careful to guard your heart. Don't hang around people who doubt. Keep your heart free from doubt and unbelief. There is going to come a time when you will have to speak to some things. Every time a mountain gets in your way, instead of turning around and running, you need to stand face-to-face and say, "Be thou removed!" Grow up in faith. Open your mouth and talk to sickness. Say, "I command this sickness to leave my body in the name of Jesus." Mark 11:23 says, "... those things which he saith" (KJV). This is not even about prayer. This is just speaking. Some stuff you have to just speak to! "He shall have whatsoever he saith" (KJV).

6. Healing through virtue or touch (Mark 5:29–30)

Jesus's virtue can be in you if you pray and fast. Luke 6:19 says, "The whole multitude sought to touch Him, for power went out from Him and healed them all." Worship is a way to reach out and touch the heart of God. True worshipers know how to get in God's presence. As you reach up in pure worship, you will be like the multitudes in Jesus's day, for "as many as touched it were made perfectly well" (Matt. 14:36). "But the hour cometh, and now is, when the true worshippers shall worship the Father in spirit and in truth: for the Father seeketh such to worship him" (John 4:23, KJV). Is this your hour?

7. Healing through the presence of God (Luke 5:17)

"The power of the Lord was present to heal them." Praise and worship is there to invite God's presence in so that people will get healed. It is not a warm-up to the message.

8. Healing through prayer (Matt. 21:22)

"All things" (KJV) includes healing. James 5:16 says that we must confess our faults and pray for one another that we may be healed. Sometimes healing doesn't come until you confess your faults and let somebody pray for you. Sometimes the key is humility.

9. Healing through the gift of healing (1 Cor. 12:9, 28)

When Jesus left the earth, He said that we would do greater works than He did. He also said that He would send a helper to instruct us and guide us in these greater works. The Holy Spirit came among men to indwell us, giving us supernatural ability to carry out the works of Christ. He accomplishes this by endowing us with various gifts that all work together to bring people into relationship with God. One of these gifts is the gift of healing.

> But the manifestation of the Spirit is given to each one for the profit of all: for to one is given the word of wisdom through the Spirit, to another the word of knowledge through the same Spirit, to another faith by the same Spirit, to another gifts of healings by the same Spirit, to another the working of miracles, to another prophecy, to another discerning of spirits, to another different kinds of tongues, to another the

interpretation of tongues. But one and the same Spirit works all these things, distributing to each one individually as He wills.... And God has appointed these in the church: first apostles, second prophets, third teachers, after that miracles, then gifts of healings, helps, administrations, varieties of tongues.

—1 Corinthians 12:7–11, 28

10. Healing through fasting (Isa. 58:8)

When you fast in the way that God leads you, He says that "your light shall break forth like the morning, your healing shall spring forth speedily, and your righteousness shall go before you; the glory of the Lord shall be your rear guard." According to this verse, you will be healed when you fast, but better yet, fasting can serve as preventative medicine. It says, "The Lord shall be your rear guard." In other words, sickness can't sneak up on you. God's got your back. While everyone else is getting swine flu, you're healthy. While there's no cure for the common cold, you sail through cold season with not so much as one symptom, sniffle, or cough.

Then there are just those times when nothing else will do except a sacrifice of going without food, a time to surrender your flesh to the Spirit of God that brings life. Jesus talks about this in Matthew 17:21: "This kind does not go out except by prayer and fasting."

11. Healing through the word (Ps. 107:20)

The Bible says that God "sent His word and healed them, and delivered them from their destructions" (Ps. 107:20). We also know that God's word does not return to Him void. It accomplishes everything for which it was sent (Isa. 55:11). If He spoke healing to you, then you are healed. Jesus said that man would not live by bread alone but by every word that proceeds out of the mouth of God. That is why learning and meditating on the Word of God is so important for your healing. Declare that by the Word of God you "shall not die, but live, and declare the works the LORD" (Ps. 118:17). Read the Word. Confess the Word. Get healing scriptures. Trust God because His word will accomplish in you all that He intends.

12. Healing through cloths/clothing (Acts 19:12)

The healing anointing is transferable. It can be in clothing. It is tangible. We pray over prayer cloths at my church, and people have been healed. Years ago while preaching in Ethiopia, I took my shirt off after ministering and cut it up into small pieces of cloth. We passed them out to all the people there, and we heard so many testimonies of healings. One person set a cloth on fire in his sick mother's home, and the smoke from the cloth healed her. She had been bedridden for years, and she got up out of her bed healed. In other countries they don't have doctors and hospitals as we do in America. They have to believe God. They are desperate for healing. They don't have all the prescription medicines, health insurance, Medicaid, and Medicare. So they come to services believing that if they don't get their healing there, they are not going to make it. They have high expectancy and high faith. God honors faith.

And when the men of that place recognized Him, they sent out into all that surrounding region, brought to Him all who were sick, and begged Him that they might only touch the hem of His garment. And as many as touched it were made perfectly well.

—Matthew 14:35–36

Now God worked unusual miracles by the hands of Paul, so that even handkerchiefs or aprons were brought from his body to the sick, and the diseases left them and the evil spirits went out of them.

—Acts 19:11–12

HEALING DECLARATIONS

By the stripes of Jesus I am healed. He took my sickness; He carried my pain. I believe it is the will of God for me to be healed.

In the name of Jesus, I break every curse of infirmity, sickness, and premature death off of my body.

In the name of Jesus, I break every curse of witchcraft and destruction over my body from both sides of my family.

In the name of Jesus, I speak to every sickness in my body and I command it to leave.

In the name of Jesus, I speak to diabetes, high blood pressure, cancer, heart attack, stroke, and multiple sclerosis. Be removed and cast into the sea.

I speak to heart, kidney, back, lung, and liver problems. Be removed and cast into the sea.

I speak to blood, skeletal, and bone conditions. Be removed and cast into the sea.

I speak to lupus and every other disease. I command you to leave my body.

Every hidden sickness and every hidden disease, I command you to leave my body in the name of Jesus.

Arthritis, pain, and rheumatism, you must go in the name of Jesus.

I command all pain to leave my body in the name of Jesus.

I come against skin conditions in the name of Jesus.

I speak to infections to come out of my body in the name of Jesus.

I speak to breathing conditions, asthma, hay fever, sinusitis, chest congestion, and pneumonia to come out of my body in the name of Jesus.

Joint conditions and pain must go in the name of Jesus.

I come against any conditions and infirmities that affect me as a woman—lupus, fibroid cysts, and tumors in the female organs.

I command those tumors to die! I loose the fire of God to burn them out in the name of Jesus.

I come against nervous conditions, insomnia, and acid reflux. God has not given me the spirit of fear, but of love, power, and a sound mind.

Heart and circulatory conditions, irregular heartbeat, angina, and stroke must leave my body. I am the temple of the Holy Spirit. Be gone in the name of Jesus.

I speak to digestive disorders and allergies to certain food. You have no place in my body. You must go in the name of Jesus.

I break any and all addictions to pain pills in the name of Jesus.

Corroded disks; slipped disks; spine, back, and neck problems—be realigned and put back in place in the name of Jesus.

I release miracles of healing in my body in the name of Jesus.

I believe God for miracles of healing in my life and in my family wherever I go in Jesus's name.

Thank You, Lord, for healing me and delivering me from all sickness and all pain in Jesus's name.

I speak to every condition: you must obey.

I speak to miracles, healings, signs, and wonders. Be released into me in Jesus's name.

I thank You, Lord, that health and healing are coming now.

CASTING OUT and RENOUNCING the SPIRIT of INFIRMITY*

Forgive me, Lord, for allowing any fear, guilt, self-rejection, self-hatred, unforgiveness, bitterness, sin, pride, or rebellion to open the door to any sickness or infirmity. I renounce these things in the name of Jesus.

Jesus carried my sickness and infirmities (Matt. 8:17).

I break, rebuke, and cast out any spirit of cancer that would attempt to establish itself in my lungs, bones, breast, throat, back, spine, liver, kidneys, pancreas, skin, or stomach in the name of Jesus.

I rebuke and cast out all spirits causing diabetes, high blood pressure, low blood pressure, heart attack, stroke, kidney failure, leukemia, blood disease, breathing problems, arthritis, lupus, Alzheimer's, or insomnia in the name of Jesus.

I cast out any spirit of infirmity that came into my life through pride in the name of Jesus.

---

* This section is taken from John Eckhardt, *Prayers That Rout Demons* (Lake Mary, FL: Charisma House, 2008), 91–95.

I cast out any spirit of infirmity that came into my life through trauma or accidents in the name of Jesus.

I cast out any spirit of infirmity that came into my life through rejection in the name of Jesus.

I cast out any spirit of infirmity that came into my life through witchcraft in the name of Jesus.

I rebuke any sickness that would come to eat up my flesh in the name of Jesus (Ps. 27:2).

I break all curses of sickness and disease, and I command all hereditary spirits of sickness to come out (Gal. 3:13).

No sickness or plague will come near my dwelling (Ps. 91:10).

I command every germ or sickness that touches my body to die in the name of Jesus.

I am redeemed from sickness and disease (Gal. 3:13).

I loose myself from every infirmity (Luke 13:12).

Chapter 1

HOW MUCH IS IT WORTH?

> And when the unclean spirit had convulsed him and cried out with a loud voice, he came out of him.... And immediately His fame spread throughout all the region around Galilee.... Now at evening, when the sun had set, they brought to Him all who were sick and those who were demon-possessed. *And the whole city was gathered together at the door.* Then He healed many who were sick with various diseases, and *cast out many demons.*
> —Mark 1:26, 28, 32–34, EMPHASIS ADDED

WHEN PEOPLE GOT word that Jesus was coming to their region, they made way to meet Him. Some traveled far on foot or donkey. Some tarried with Him for days on end with no food. Some who were crippled or maimed were carried into town by friends and family. One person's friends tore up somebody's roof and lowered him into the house Jesus was visiting. Multitudes of people pressed and prodded against each other at the risk of being trampled just to get close to Jesus. Their healing, deliverance, and hunger for the Word were so valuable to them that they put their lives on hold and safety at risk. They knew that if they could just get into Jesus's presence, all their worries would be subsided and their needs met.

How much is your healing worth to you? Are you willing to travel long distances, go without food, brave large crowds, and do whatever it takes to get to the place where the anointing is active and effective?

People came to hear Jesus because He created a demand by setting people free. When people hear of miracles, they will gather to hear the Word of God. They will come with expectancy and faith and draw from the anointing of the servant of God. *There is no substitute for miracles.* They will cause a hunger to come into the hearts of people. Hungry hearts will always gather and put a demand on the anointing.

If we want hungry people, we must have miracles. Some churches wonder why their people are so unconcerned and apathetic about serving God. People drag to service. Some pastors will try all kinds of programs to raise the excitement of the people, but there is no substitute for doing it God's way. Where there are miracles, there will be people gathered. Miracles increase the authenticity of our salvation, and people come to value the presence of God more and more. Faith levels rise when miracles happen.

> And straightway many were gathered together, inso-
> much that there was no room to receive them, no, not
> so much as about the door: and he preached the word
> unto them.
>
> —Mark 2:2, KJV

As people gathered to hear the Word, there was not enough room. This was the result of "His fame spread abroad throughout all the region around Galilee." I like ministering in packed houses. When a church is filled up, there is a higher level of expectancy and faith among the people. It shows how much the people in that area value the anointing and how much they desire to be healed. When a church is half empty, it seems to be harder to minister. We need the anointing to build churches—but we also need the anointing to fill them. I have been to churches that seated a thousand and only a hundred showed up.

Some only show up because the pastor tells them to, or they are just in the habit of going to church. Miracles, prophecies, and healing will not flow out of the servant of God to the extent that they will where there is a demand. Of course, a minister can stir up the gifts of God and minister by faith. However, when the faith of the people is high, it is much easier to minister. The giving and receiving of the anointing is a give-and-take relationship. The more you want to receive and the more value it has for you, the more you will demand it and draw from it, and the more the Holy Spirit will flood the minister with the anointing so that all who are touched will be healed.

Jesus could, in His own hometown, do no *mighty* work because of their unbelief. Unbelief hinders the flow of the anointing. Faith releases the flow. Unbelievers will not put a demand on the anointing, but believers will.

The more people hear and are taught about the anointing, the greater will be their capacity to put a demand on it. As a pastor of a local church, I teach the members about different gifts and anointings. When I teach about the gift of healing, this builds their faith for healing. When ministers come to minister at our church, I tell the members about the anointing on the person's life. They then have the responsibility to draw from and put a demand on that anointing by their faith.

You will find that most of the people who received miracles from Jesus either came or were brought to Him. Many beseeched Him.

> And it came to pass, that the father of Publius lay sick of a fever and of a bloody flux: to whom Paul entered in, and prayed, and laid his hands on him, and healed him. So when this was done, others also, which had diseases in the island, came, and were healed: who also honoured us with many honours; and when we departed, they laded us with such things as were necessary.
>
> —Acts 28:8–10, KJV

After the father of Publius was healed, the whole island of Melita came to be healed. That one miracle increased the value of Paul's anointing. It caused the people to do whatever they could to get some of what Paul had. Notice, they honored Paul with many honors. Honoring the servant of God is a key to receiving from the anointing in his or her life. We will talk more about honor in a later chapter. The scripture states that the people came. They came with the sick, expecting to be healed. They put action on their faith and came.

Passive, apathetic saints do not receive from the anointing.

We cannot be passive and expect to receive from these gifts. We must be active with our faith. People have to have a hunger and thirst for the things of the Spirit. Hungry souls will always draw from the anointing.

How much is your healing worth to you? How far will you follow the leading of God to capitalize on all He has for you?

PRAYERS THAT INCREASE HUNGER FOR THE HEALING ANOINTING

O God, let me see You face-to-face so that my life will be preserved (Gen. 32:30–31).

I will follow the instructions of the man of God, so that my body is restored like that of a little child and I will be clean (2 Kings 5:14).

I declare that it is well with my family and me, no matter what it looks like to my natural eyes. I will go and seek out the man of God that he may stretch his anointing over the dead places in our health. He will breathe into us, and we will rise up to new life (2 Kings 4:8–37).

I will follow You, Lord Jesus. I cry out to You, "Son of David, have mercy on me!" I believe that You are able to heal me and restore me. Touch me and let it be to me according to my faith (Matt. 9:27–30).

Son of David, have mercy on me and do not send me away. I have come from a far region crying out to You for healing.

I worship You, O Lord. Help me! I am hungry for even the crumbs that fall from Your table. Let my healing come to me as I desire (Matt. 15:22–28).

Jesus, I come to You in the midst of the multitude. I am hungrier for Your healing than for food. I feel Your compassion for me and know that You will heal me (Matt. 15:30–33).

I will fast according to Your leading. Then I know that my healing will break forth like the morning. My healing will spring forth speedily (Isa. 58:6–8).

I have walked before You, O Lord, in truth and with a loyal heart. I have done what is good in Your sight. I weep bitterly before You. I know You have heard my prayer and have seen my tears. Surely You will heal me (2 Kings 20:3–5).

I humble myself before You, O God. I pray and seek Your face. I turn from my wicked ways. Then I know You will hear from heaven. You will forgive my sin and heal me (2 Chron. 7:14).

Have mercy on me, O Lord, for I am weak. Heal me, for my bones are troubled (Ps. 6:2).

Lord, be merciful to me and heal my soul (Ps. 41:4).

I declare that this is my time to be healed (Eccles. 3:3).

You have seen my ways and will heal me. You will also lead me and restore comforts to my mourners and to me (Isa. 57:18).

Words of praise are on my lips. May peace be unto me, for the Lord will heal me (Isa. 57:19).

Heal me, O Lord, and I will be healed. Save me and I will be saved. You are my praise (Jer. 17:14).

You will restore health to me and heal me of all my wounds (Jer. 30:17).

You will bring health and healing to me. You will heal me and reveal to me the abundance of peace and truth (Jer. 33:6).

You have said, "I will come and heal him" (Matt. 8:7).

The power of the Lord is present to heal me (Luke 5:17).

Let news of Your healing power, O Lord, be like a ripple effect, causing all those near and far to come so that they will be healed (Acts 28:8–10).

Let many gather together so that there be no more room to receive them, that they may hear the preaching of the Word and be healed (Mark 2:2).

I will press against the crowds, fight my way through traffic, and let no one stop me until I get into Your presence. If only I can touch the hem of Your garment, I know I will be made whole (Mark 5:27–28).

I hunger and thirst for Your righteousness, and I know I will be filled (Matt. 5:6).

HEALING BY PUTTING AWAY ANGER, BITTERNESS, AND UNFORGIVENESS

ANGER

I will cease from anger and put away wrath to stay connected to God. If I wait on Him, I will inherit the earth (Ps. 37:8–9).

My whole body is sick, and my health is broken because of my sins. But I confess my sins and am deeply sorry for what I have done. Do not abandon me, O Lord. Come quickly to help me, O Lord my Savior (Ps. 38:3, 18, 22, NLT).

I will speak soft words, kind words, and words of life to turn wrath and anger away from me. I will not grieve anyone with my words (Prov. 15:1).

I will appease the strife against my health and my family by being slow to anger (Prov. 15:18).

I am better than the mighty because I control my anger. There is more gain in ruling my spirit than conquering a city (Prov. 16:32).

I use discretion to defer my anger; I earn esteem by overlooking wrongs (Prov. 19:11).

I will not sin against my own soul by provoking the King to anger (Prov. 20:2).

I will silence anger with a secret gift (Prov. 21:14).

I declare that anger's reign in my life will come to an end (Prov. 22:8).

I cast out the cruelty and destruction of wrath and anger. They will not flood my emotions any longer (Prov. 27:4).

I will be slow to anger and will keep its clutches from resting in my bosom (Eccles. 7:9).

Let all wrath and anger be put away from me (Eph. 4:31).

I am a new person, having been renewed after the image of Him who created me; therefore, I put off anger (Col. 3:8–10).

I will not discourage my children by provoking them to anger (Col. 3:21).

BITTERNESS

Lord, I give the bitterness of my soul to You. Please look upon my affliction and remember me. I will go in peace because You have granted my petition (1 Sam. 1:10–11, 17).

I will speak openly to You, O Lord, and release all of my bitterness to You (Job 7:11).

I will speak to You, God, in the bitterness of my soul. I will find the root of why my spirit contends with Yours (Job 10:1–2).

I declare that I will not die in the bitterness of my soul, and I will eat with pleasure (Job 21:25).

My heart knows its own bitterness (Prov. 14:10); I release it to You.

I will raise wise children who will cause me no grief or bitterness (Prov. 17:25).

I had great bitterness, but in love You delivered me from the pit of corruption. For You have put all my sins behind Your back (Isa. 38:17).

I was in bitterness and in the heat of my spirit, but the hand of the Lord is strong upon me (Ezek. 3:14).

I repent of my wickedness and pray to God that the thoughts of my heart be forgiven, for I am bound by bitterness and iniquity (Acts 8:21–23).

My mouth is full of cursing and bitterness, but You have shown me a better way and I have been made right in Your sight (Rom. 3:14, 21–22).

I diligently look within myself so that I will not be defiled by any root of bitterness that may spring up (Heb. 12:15).

FORGIVENESS

I will go to my brother and ask that he forgive me of my trespasses against him (Gen. 50:17).

I pray that my brother will forgive me so that when I go before God, He will take this death away from me (Exod. 10:17).

Like Moses, I come to You asking Your forgiveness on behalf of Your people and myself. Thank You, God, that You forgive all those who sin against You, for You have blotted them out of Your book (Exod. 32:32–33).

God, I thank You that when You hear our prayers You also forgive us (1 Kings 8:30).

You have heard from heaven, forgiven my sin, and have delivered me into the land You promised my fathers (1 Kings 8:34).

You have heard from heaven, forgiven my sin, and have taught me the good way in which I should walk (1 Kings 8:36).

You have heard from heaven, forgiven my sin, and will do and give me according to my ways because You know my heart (1 Kings 8:39).

Forgive me of my sins, and have compassion upon me (1 Kings 8:50).

I am called by Your name and have humbled myself before You. I pray and seek Your face and have turned from my wicked ways. Now You will hear from heaven and forgive my sin and heal me (2 Chron. 7:14).

Look upon my affliction and my pain, and forgive all my sins (Ps. 25:18).

You, O Lord, are good and ready to forgive. Your mercy is plentiful to all those who call on You (Ps. 86:5).

The Lord declares that He will forgive my iniquity and remember my sin no more (Jer. 31:34).

O Lord, hear. O Lord, forgive. O Lord, listen and do! For I am called by Your name (Dan. 9:19).

As I forgive others, Lord, I pray that You will forgive me (Matt. 6:12).

I will forgive those who have wronged me, because if I don't, God will not forgive me (Matt. 6:14–15).

You have healed me and said, "Arise and take up your bed," so that I will know that You have the power to forgive sins on Earth (Matt. 9:6).

Like the servant who owed the king ten thousand talents, I too have been forgiven much. Therefore, I will go and forgive all those who have sinned against me so that I will not be given over to the tormentors (Matt. 18:23–35).

I will forgive any person with whom I have ought, so that when I stand praying, my Father in heaven will forgive me also (Mark 11:25).

If I forgive others, I will be forgiven (Luke 6:37).

Forgive me of my sins because I also have forgiven all those whom I felt were indebted to me. Keep me from temptation, and deliver me from evil (Luke 11:4).

If my brother hurts me, I will tell him that he hurt me. Then if he asks for forgiveness, I will forgive him. If he continues to hurt me and asks for forgiveness each time, I will forgive him every time (Luke 17:3–4).

With Jesus, I pray, "Father, forgive them, for they do not know what they do" (Luke 23:34).

I declare that Satan will not get an advantage over me, because I walk in forgiveness just as Christ did. I am not ignorant of the devil's devices (2 Cor. 2:10–11).

I confess my sins before God, and I know that God is faithful and just to forgive me and to cleanse me from all unrighteousness (1 John 1:9).

I confess my faults to my fellow believers, and we pray for one another so that we will be healed, because the earnest prayer of a righteous person has great power and wonderful results (James 5:16).

I have been sent to the Gentiles to open their eyes, turn them from darkness to light, and deliver them from the power of Satan, so that they may receive forgiveness (Acts 26:18).

Through Christ's blood, I have been redeemed and have received forgiveness for my sins and riches according to His grace (Eph. 1:7).

Father God, you have delivered me from the power of darkness and translated me into the kingdom of Your Son in whom I have been redeemed and forgiven of all my sins (Col. 1:13–14).

HEALING THROUGH OBEDIENCE

I will obey the voice of my Father according to all He has commanded me (Gen. 27:8).

I will arise and obey Your voice and flee from my enemies (Gen. 27:43–44).

I have a special treasure in the Lord because I obey His voice and keep His covenant (Exod. 19:5).

I will obey the voice of the angel of the Lord to keep me in the right way and bring me to a place that God Himself has prepared for me (Exod. 23:20).

I will obey the angel of the Lord, for he will not pardon my sin because the name of the Lord is in him (Exod. 23:21).

As I obey the angel of the Lord and do all that God has spoken through him, my enemies will be God's enemies (Exod. 23:22).

I am blessed because I obey the commandments of the Lord (Deut. 11:27).

I will walk after the Lord my God and fear Him, keep His commandments and obey Him. I will serve Him and cleave to Him (Deut. 13:4).

I will obey the voice of the Lord my God and do all of His commandments and statutes that He has commanded me this day (Deut. 27:10).

I will be left in number if I do not obey the voice of the Lord (Deut. 28:62).

I will return to the Lord my God. I will obey His voice according to all He commands me. With all my heart and soul, from generation to generation, my children and I will obey God. Then the Lord will set us free from any captivity of the enemy, and He will have compassion on us (Deut. 30:2–3).

The Lord my God will put curses on all my enemies because I obey His voice and do all that He has commanded me (Deut. 30:7–8).

The Lord my God will make me plenteous in all the work of my hand, in the fruit of my body, and in the fruit of my land. He will rejoice over me because I obey Him and hearken to His voice (Deut. 30:9–10).

I obey the voice of the Lord, for He is my life, and in Him are the length of days (Deut. 30:20).

I will serve the Lord my God, and His voice I will obey (Josh. 24:24).

I will not refuse to obey the voice of the prophet of God (1 Sam. 8:19).

I will fear the Lord, serve Him, and obey His voice. I will not rebel against the commandments of the Lord. The hand of the Lord is with me (1 Sam. 12:14–15).

My obedience to the voice of the Lord is better than any sacrifice (1 Sam. 15:22).

I will not be like the fathers of Israel. I will be humble and submit to obeying the Lord. I will be mindful of the wonders that God does on my behalf, for He is gracious and merciful, ready to pardon, slow to anger, and of great kindness. He has not forsaken me (Neh. 9:16–17).

I will spend my days in prosperity and my years in pleasures. I will not perish and die without knowledge, because I obey and serve the Lord (Job 36:11–12).

As soon as I heard of the Lord, I submitted myself to Him and obeyed (Ps. 18:44).

The ravens shall not pluck out my eye, neither shall the young eagles eat it. I do not mock my Father, neither do I despise to obey my mother (Prov. 30:17).

I will obey Your voice, and You will be my God. I will walk in all the ways that You have commanded me, and it will be well with me (Jer. 7:23).

I will obey the voice of the Lord, and He will give to me the land that He swore to my fathers—a land flowing with milk and honey (Jer. 11:4–5).

You have risen early, O God, and have pleaded with me, "Obey My voice" (Jer. 11:7).

Lord, You have said that if I do not obey You, You will pluck me up and destroy me (Jer. 12:17).

If I do not obey You, You will withdraw the good that You have extended to me (Jer. 18:10).

I will amend my ways and my doings. I will obey the voice of the Lord my God, and the Lord will relinquish the evil that He had pronounced against me (Jer. 26:13).

I will obey the voice of the Lord so that it will be well with me and my soul will live (Jer. 38:20).

Whether I like it or not, I will obey the voice of the Lord my God, that it may be well with me (Jer. 42:6, NLT).

Kingdoms and dominions shall be given to me because I obey and serve the Most High (Dan. 7:27).

I have transgressed the law and departed from God by not obeying His voice. Now a curse has been poured on me and the oath that God made to me (Dan. 9:11).

Those who are far off shall come and build the temple of the Lord, because I diligently obey the voice of the Lord my God (Zech. 6:15).

I declare that as the winds and seas obeyed Jesus, the winds and seas that rise up in my life will obey me (Matt. 8:27).

With authority I will command even the unclean spirits and they will obey me (Mark 1:27).

All those who surround me will fear exceedingly, saying to one another, "What kind of person is this that even the wind and the sea obey him?" (Mark 4:41).

With my mustard seed of faith, I will speak to the mulberry tree and command it to be plucked up by the root and planted in the sea, and it will obey me (Luke 17:6).

I obey God rather than man (Acts 5:29).

God has given me the Holy Spirit because I obey Him (Acts 5:32).

I will not be like the fathers of Israel who would not obey but rejected the man of God and turned their hearts back to Egypt (Acts 7:39).

Let me not be like those who obey unrighteousness, indignation, and wrath, for tribulation and anguish is their portion (Rom. 2:8–9).

Let no sin reign in my body that I should obey its lusts (Rom. 6:12).

Whatever I submit myself to obey, I am slave to it, whether it be sin unto death or God unto righteousness (Rom. 6:16).

I cast off the enemy of my soul, who tries to bewitch me that I should not obey the truth. Before my eyes Jesus Christ has been clearly portrayed before me as crucified (Gal. 3:1).

Let me not run well, then find out at the end that someone or something hindered me from obeying the truth (Gal. 5:7).

My children will obey and honor their father and mother so that it will be well with them and that they may live long on the earth (Eph. 6:1–3).

My children obey me in all things because this is well pleasing to the Lord (Col. 3:20).

I will obey those for whom I work, not with eye service or as a man pleaser, but with sincerity of heart, fearing God (Col. 3:22).

I know God and obey the gospel of the Lord Jesus Christ; therefore, I will not be punished with everlasting destruction and banished from the presence of the Lord and the glory of His power (2 Thess. 1:7–9).

If I do not obey the word of the apostles, I will have no company with the people of God and I will be ashamed (2 Thess. 3:14).

Let me be reminded to be subject to rulers and authorities, to obey, to be ready for every good work, to speak evil of no one, to be peaceable and gentle, showing all humility to all men (Titus 3:1–2).

Let me be a son like Christ, who learned obedience by the things He suffered and was made perfect (Heb. 5:8–9).

I will obey those who have rule over me. I will submit myself to them because they watch out for my soul, as those who must give account (Heb. 13:17).

Like we put bridles in the horse's mouth, let me bridle my whole body that it may obey (James 3:2–3).

Let the wife be subject to her own husband so that even if he is not obedient to the Word, he may be won by the conduct of his wife (1 Pet. 3:1).

For the time has come that judgment must begin at the house of God. And if it first begins with us, what will the end be of those who do not obey the gospel of God (1 Pet. 4:17)?

I have received grace and discipleship from Jesus Christ my Lord so that I can be obedient to the faith among the nations for His name (Rom. 1:3–6).

Jesus, I thank You that by Your obedience many have been made righteous (Rom. 5:19).

My obedience has become known to all, but I still must remain wise in what is right and simple concerning evil (Rom. 16:19).

The mystery of the gospel is now made manifest and made known to all nations for the obedience of faith (Rom. 16:26).

The man of God has greater affection for me because he remembers my obedience (2 Cor. 7:15).

I cast down imaginations and every high thing that exalts itself against the knowledge of God, and I bring into captivity every thought to the obedience of Christ (2 Cor. 10:5).

I punish all disobedience when my obedience is fulfilled (2 Cor. 10:6).

I have been elected according to the foreknowledge of God the Father and sanctified with His Spirit for obedience, and have been sprinkled with the blood of Jesus Christ (1 Pet. 1:2).

HEALING THROUGH WISDOM, KNOWLEDGE, and UNDERSTANDING

I have been filled with the spirit of wisdom (Exod. 28:3).

I am filled with the Spirit of God, in wisdom, understanding, knowledge, and all manner of workmanship to design artistic works (Exod. 31:3–4).

I have been filled with wisdom of heart to do all manner of work (Exod. 35:35).

I have been brought to the sanctuary of the Lord with other wise-hearted men, for the Lord has put wisdom and understanding to know how to do all manner of work for the service of the sanctuary according to all the Lord has commanded (Exod. 36:1).

I will be careful to observe the statutes of the Lord, for they are my wisdom and understanding in the sight of the nations, who will hear them and say, "Surely you are wise and understanding," for who is the person that God is so near that I may call upon Him for any reason? (Deut. 4:6–7).

Like Joshua the son of Nun, I am full of the spirit of wisdom (Deut. 34:9).

I am wise, according to the wisdom of the angel of the Lord, to know all the things that are in the earth (2 Sam. 14:20).

The wisdom of God is in me to administer justice (1 Kings 3:28).

Like Solomon, God has given me wisdom, exceedingly great understanding, and a heart as large as the sand on the seashore (1 Kings 4:29).

My wisdom excels the wisdom of men (1 Kings 4:30).

Because the wisdom of God is in me, people will come to hear my wisdom, even the kings of the earth (1 Kings 4:34).

The Lord has given me the wisdom He had promised to me, as He did with Solomon (1 Kings 5:12).

Because of the wisdom of God upon my life, people will come from all around to see the true report of my acts and wisdom and prosperity. People who work with me are happy and will stand before me continually to hear the wisdom of God (1 Kings 10:6–8).

Because of the wisdom of God upon my life, my riches and wisdom will exceed all the kings of the earth. People will seek out my wisdom, which God has put in my heart (1 Kings 10:23–24).

Only the Lord gives me wisdom and understanding that I may keep the law of the Lord my God (1 Chron. 22:12).

Give me now wisdom and knowledge that I may go out before Your people (2 Chron. 1:10).

Because it was in my heart to ask God for wisdom and knowledge that I may serve God's people, and not riches, wealth, honor, the life of my enemies, or long life, wisdom and knowledge have been granted to me (2 Chron. 1:11–12).

After the wisdom of my God that is set in my hand, I will set magistrates and judges for the people of God, so that they may know the laws of God (Ezra 7:25).

May I not die without wisdom (Job 4:21).

May God show me the secrets of wisdom, for they double my prudence (Job 11:6).

Let me be like the aged men, for wisdom, understanding, and strength are with them (Job 12:12–13).

With the Lord are strength and wisdom (Job 12:16).

The price of wisdom is above rubies (Job 28:18).

I fear the Lord, for in that is wisdom, and to depart from evil is understanding (Job 28:28).

Age speaks to me, and the multitude of years teaches me wisdom (Job 32:7).

God, You are mighty in strength and wisdom (Job 36:5).

God, only You can put wisdom in my mind or give understanding to my heart (Job 38:36).

I am made righteous; therefore, my mouth speaks wisdom and my tongue talks of justice (Ps. 37:30).

My mouth will speak of wisdom, and the meditation of my heart will be understanding (Ps. 49:3).

You, O Lord, desire truth in my inward parts, and in the hidden part You will make me know wisdom (Ps. 51:6).

Teach me to number my days so that I may apply my heart to wisdom (Ps. 90:12).

How manifold are Your works, O Lord. In wisdom You have made them all. The earth is full of Your possessions (Ps. 104:24).

I will fear the Lord, for in that is the beginning of wisdom, and all those who do His commandments have good understanding (Ps. 111:10).

I will know wisdom and instruction. I will perceive words of understanding (Prov. 1:2).

I receive the instruction of wisdom, justice, judgment, and equity (Prov. 1:3).

I am wise; therefore, I will hear and increase my learning. I am a person of understanding; therefore, I will attain wise counsel to understand a proverb and its interpretation and the words of the wise and their riddles (Prov. 2:5–6).

I will fear the Lord, for in that is the beginning of knowledge. I will not be a fool who despises wisdom and instruction (Prov. 2:7).

I will turn to the reproof and cries of wisdom. I will not be simpleminded or delight in scorning. I will not be like the fool who hates knowledge, but I will receive wisdom that pours its spirit out upon me. I will receive the words that it has made known to me (Prov. 1:20–23).

I incline my ear to wisdom and apply my heart to understanding (Prov. 2:2).

I cry out for discernment and lift up my voice for understanding. I seek after it as if it were silver or a hidden treasure. Now I know that I will understand the fear of the Lord, and I will find the knowledge of God, because He gives wisdom, knowledge, and understanding out of His mouth (Prov. 2:3–6).

God has stored up wisdom for me, and He shields me because I walk uprightly (Prov. 2:7).

Wisdom has entered my heart, and knowledge is pleasant to my soul. Now discretion preserves me and understanding keeps me, delivering me from the way of evil and from the man who speaks perverse things (Prov. 2:10–12).

I am happy because I have found wisdom and understanding, for it is better than the profits of silver, and its gain than fine gold. Wisdom is more precious than rubies, and nothing I have can be compared to it (Prov. 3:13–15).

Length of days is in the right hand of wisdom, and riches and honor are in the left. The ways of wisdom are pleasant, and all her paths are peace (Prov. 3:16–17).

I lay hold of wisdom, for she is a tree of life to me, and I am happy when I retain her (Prov. 3:18).

By wisdom, the Lord founded the earth, by understanding He established the heavens, and by knowledge the depths are broken up and the clouds drop dew (Prov. 3:19–20).

I will not let sound wisdom or discretion depart from my eyes, for they are life to my soul and grace to my neck. With them,

I walk safely in my way, and my foot does not stumble (Prov. 3:21–23).

I will get wisdom and understanding. I will not forget nor will I turn away from the words of Your mouth. I will not forsake wisdom because she preserves me. I will love her, and she will keep me (Prov. 4:5–6).

Wisdom is the principal thing; therefore, I will get wisdom. And with all my getting, I will get understanding (Prov. 4:7).

I am promoted because I exalt wisdom (Prov. 4:8).

Honor comes to me because I love wisdom (Prov. 4:8).

An ornament of grace and a crown of glory are placed upon my head because I embrace wisdom (Prov. 4:9).

You have taught me in the way of wisdom and have led me in the right paths. When I walk, my steps are not hindered. When I run, I do not stumble (Prov. 4:11–12).

I pay attention to the wisdom of the Lord. I lend my ear to His understanding so that I may preserve discretion and my lips will keep knowledge (Prov. 5:1–2).

I love wisdom like a sister, and insight is a beloved member of my family. They hold me back from immoral behavior and from listening to the flattery of strangers (Prov. 7:4–5, NLT).

Wisdom cries out to me, and understanding lifts up her voice so that I can hear (Prov. 8:1).

I am of a prudent and understanding heart (Prov. 8:5).

I speak of excellent things, and from the opening of my lips are right things. My mouth speaks truth, and wickedness is an abomination to my lips. All the words of my mouth are righteous. There is nothing crooked or perverse in them, because I operate with the spirit of wisdom (Prov. 8:6–8).

The words of wisdom are all plain to me because I have understanding; they are right to me because I have knowledge (Prov. 8:9).

I receive wise instruction and not silver, and knowledge rather than choice gold (Prov. 8:10).

For wisdom is better than rubies, and nothing that I desire can compare to it (Prov. 8:11).

Because I have wisdom I dwell with prudence and find out knowledge and discretion (Prov. 8:12).

Because I have wisdom, counsel and sound wisdom are mine. I am understanding, and I have strength (Prov. 8:14).

I have the beginnings of wisdom because I fear the Lord, and the knowledge of His holiness is understanding (Prov. 9:10).

Wisdom is found in my lips because I have understanding (Prov. 10:13).

I store up knowledge because I am a wise person (Prov. 10:14).

I am not a fool who dies in want of wisdom, but the words from my mouth feed many (Prov. 10:21).

I am person of understanding; therefore, I have wisdom (Prov. 10:23).

My mouth brings forth wisdom (Prov. 10:31).

I am humble, and wisdom is with me (Prov. 11:2).

As a person who has wisdom and understanding, I hold my peace (Prov. 11:12).

Let me be commended according to my wisdom, but I keep my heart from perversion so that I will not be despised (Prov. 12:8).

I till my land and am satisfied with bread. Yet if I follow after frivolity, I will be void of understanding (Prov. 12:11).

Wisdom is with me because I am well advised (Prov. 13:10).

Knowledge and wisdom come easily to me because I have understanding (Prov. 14:6).

I will leave the presence of foolish people when I do not perceive in them the lips of knowledge (Prov. 14:7).

My wisdom is in understanding my way (Prov. 14:8).

Wisdom rests in my heart because I have understanding (Prov. 14:33).

I walk uprightly because I have understanding (Prov. 15:21).

I am instructed of wisdom because I fear the Lord (Prov. 15:33).

It is much better that I have chosen wisdom rather than gold, and understanding rather than silver (Prov. 16:16).

I will not be like the man void of understanding and agree to secure a friend's debt (Prov. 17:18).

I set my sights on wisdom because I have understanding (Prov. 17:24).

I spare my words and have a calm spirit, because I have knowledge and understanding (Prov. 17:27).

I hold my peace and keep my lips shut; even then I appear wise and perceptive (Prov. 17:28).

I will not be like the man who isolates himself and seeks his own desire, raging against wise judgment, for he is a fool who does not delight in understanding but delights in expressing his own heart (Prov. 18:1–2).

The words of my mouth are like life-giving water. In it are words of true wisdom that are as refreshing as a bubbling brook (Prov. 18:4, NLT).

I am one who gets wisdom because I love my own soul. I will keep understanding so that I will find good (Prov. 19:8).

None of my human wisdom, understanding, or counsel can stand against the Lord (Prov. 21:30).

I will not overwork myself to become rich. I must cease from trying in my own understanding (Prov. 23:4).

I will not speak in the hearing of a fool, because he will despise the wisdom of my words (Prov. 23:9).

I will buy truth, wisdom, instruction, and understanding and will never sell them (Prov. 23:23).

Through wisdom my house is built, and by understanding it is established. By knowledge the rooms will be filled with all precious and pleasant riches (Prov. 24:3–4).

I am strong because I am wise and full of knowledge (Prov. 24:5).

Let me not be like the fool for whom wisdom is too much, but let me be able to speak wisely in the presence of leaders (Prov. 24:7, NLT).

The knowledge of wisdom is my reward, and my expectations for it have been surpassed (Prov. 24:14).

My father rejoices in me because I love wisdom, and I do not keep company with immoral people (Prov. 29:3).

I receive the rod of correction, for it imparts wisdom, but I disgrace my mother if I am left to myself (Prov. 29:15, NIV).

I open my mouth with wisdom, and on my tongue is the law of kindness (Prov. 31:26).

I have given my heart to seek and search out wisdom concerning all things that are done under heaven (Eccles. 1:13).

I see that wisdom excels folly and light excels darkness, for my eyes are in my head but a fool walks around in darkness (Eccles. 2:13–14).

I am good in the sight of the Lord, for He gives me wisdom, knowledge, and joy (Eccles. 2:26).

The wisdom that God gives me is good with an inheritance, and both wisdom and money are a defense, but only wisdom gives me life (Eccles. 7:11–12).

I am stronger than ten mighty men because I have wisdom (Eccles. 7:19).

I am wise and able to analyze and interpret things. Wisdom lights up my face and softens the hardness of my countenance (Eccles. 8:1, NLT).

Day and night I applied my heart to know wisdom and to see the business that is done on the earth. It was then that I beheld all the work of God (Eccles. 8:16–17).

I deliver whole cities with my wisdom, for wisdom is better than strength and weapons of war (Eccles. 9:15–18).

I will not give in to even a little folly else my reputation for wisdom and honor will send forth a foul odor (Eccles. 10:1).

My heart leads me to do right because I am wise (Eccles. 10:2).

Let the wisdom of God bring me success (Eccles. 10:10).

Let me not be like the king of Assyria, thinking that by the strength of my hands I have done it, or by my own wisdom I am prudent (Isa. 10:13). For it is the Lord my God who makes me strong and wise.

The Spirit of the Lord rests upon me, and the spirit of wisdom and understanding, the spirit of counsel and might, the spirit of knowledge, and the fear of the Lord also rest on me because my delight is the fear of the Lord (Isa. 11:2–3).

Wisdom and knowledge are my stability in these times. They are the strength of my salvation, and the fear of the Lord is my treasure (Isa. 33:6).

I will not reject the word of the Lord, for what wisdom is there in that? (Jer. 8:9).

I do not glory in my own wisdom, might, or riches, but I glory in knowing and understanding the Lord. He is the I AM, who exercises loving-kindness, judgment, and righteousness in the earth. In these things I do delight (Jer. 9:23–24).

I thank You, Lord, for You have made the earth by Your power, established the world by Your wisdom, and stretched out the heavens by Your understanding (Jer. 51:15). I know that You will extend Your power, wisdom, and understanding to heal me.

Let it not be to me that I get rich through my own wisdom and understanding. Let my heart not be lifted up because of worldly riches (Ezek. 28:4–5), but let me humbly receive the wisdom and understanding that God gives, so that I will be made whole—body, mind, and spirit.

Let it not be to me that strangers or the most terrible of nations come upon me to draw their swords against the beauty of my wisdom and defile me (Ezek. 28:7), but let me be wrapped in humility and covered by the mighty hand of the only wise God so that all of His promises to heal me will come to pass.

Like Daniel, I am presented before the king as a child with no blemish. I am well favored and gifted in all wisdom, possessing knowledge, and quick to understand (Dan. 1:4).

Like Daniel and his friends, God has given me knowledge and skill in learning and wisdom and understanding in all dreams and visions (Dan. 1:17).

In all matters of wisdom and understanding, I am found ten times better than all the magicians and astrologers in this realm (Dan. 1:20), for by His might God has empowered me with His Spirit and healed my mind.

Like Daniel, I will answer those who inquire of me with counsel and wisdom (Dan. 2:14).

With Daniel I bless the name of God forever and ever, for wisdom and might are His. He changes the times and seasons; He removes kings and sets them up. He gives wisdom to the wise and knowledge to them who have understanding. He reveals deep and secret things; He knows what is in the darkness, and light dwells with Him (Dan. 2:20–22).

I thank You and praise You, God of my fathers, for You have given me wisdom and might. You have made known to me what I have asked of You (Dan. 2:23).

Secret things have not been revealed to me to show that I am wiser than anyone else, but they have been revealed to benefit the people so that they will understand what is in their own hearts (Dan. 2:30).

Kings and rulers will hear of me and the Spirit of God that dwells in me. They will know that light, understanding, and excellent wisdom are found in me (Dan. 5:14).

I will listen for the voice of the Lord that cries out in my city. I will fear His name because I am wise. I will heed the rod and the One who appointed it (Mic. 6:9, NIV).

Like the queen of the south, I will arise from wherever I am to hear the wisdom of the One greater than Solomon (Matt. 12:42).

Like Jesus, I have been sent out to teach in my own city, and they will ask, "Where did this person get such wisdom and these miraculous powers?" (Matt. 13:54).

Many will wonder where my wisdom and gifts of teaching, healing, and miracles come from (Mark 6:2), and they will know that they come from the Lord God who has healed me.

Like Jesus, I go forth in the spirit and power of Elijah to turn the disobedient to the wisdom of the just (Luke 1:17).

I grow and am strong in spirit, filled with wisdom, and the grace of God is upon me (Luke 2:40).

Like Jesus, I increase in wisdom and stature and in favor with God and man (Luke 2:52).

The fruit of my life shows the wisdom of God that dwells in me (Luke 7:35).

For the Lord will give me a mouth and wisdom, which none of my adversaries will be able to contradict or resist (Luke 21:15).

I am a person of good reputation, full of the Holy Spirit and wisdom (Acts 6:3).

Those who rise up in dispute against me will not be able to resist the wisdom and the Spirit by which I speak (Acts 6:9–10).

Like Joseph, God has delivered me from all my afflictions. He has given me favor and wisdom (Acts 7:10).

Like Moses, I am learned in all wisdom and am mighty in words and deeds (Acts 7:22).

O God, how deep are the riches of Your wisdom and knowledge! Your judgments are unsearchable, and Your ways are past finding out (Rom. 11:33).

I will not be wise according to the flesh, for God has chosen the foolish things of the world to put the wise to shame, the weak things to shame the mighty. No flesh will glory in His presence. I glory in the Lord (1 Cor. 1:26–31).

I do not come with excellent speech or my own wisdom, for I am determined to know nothing else except Jesus Christ and Him crucified (1 Cor. 2:1–2).

My speech and my preaching are not with persuasive words of human wisdom but in demonstration of the Spirit and power, that faith will stand in God and not in the wisdom of men (1 Cor. 2:4–5).

I speak wisdom among those who are mature, but not wisdom of this world or of the princes of this world. I speak the wisdom of God that He ordained before the world for our benefit (1 Cor. 2:6–7).

The things I speak are not in the words of man's wisdom, but those that the Holy Spirit teaches, comparing spiritual things with spiritual (1 Cor. 2:13).

The wisdom I have is not the wisdom of this world, for it is foolishness with God. Therefore, I do not glory in men, because all things are God's (1 Cor. 3:19, 21).

Let it be that I profit from the gifts of the Spirit, for He gives to one the word of wisdom and to another the word of knowledge (1 Cor. 12:8).

I am conducting myself in the world with simplicity and godly sincerity, not with fleshly wisdom but by the grace of God (2 Cor. 1:12).

God has poured out to me all wisdom and prudence, having made known to me the mystery of His will, according to His good pleasure (Eph. 1:8–9).

May God give me the spirit of wisdom and revelation in the knowledge of Him. Let the eyes of my understanding be enlightened so I will know the hope of His calling and the riches of the glory of His inheritance (Eph. 1:17–18).

I preach among the Gentiles the unsearchable riches of Christ with the intention of making known the manifold wisdom of God to the principalities and powers in the heavenly places (Eph. 3:8, 11).

I preach Christ, the hope of all glory, warning every man and teaching them in all wisdom so that they may be presented perfect in Christ Jesus (Col. 1:28).

I will not impose upon myself religious regulations, for in them are the appearance of wisdom, humility, and neglect of the body, but they have no value against the indulgence of the flesh (Col. 2:23).

Let the Word of Christ dwell in me richly in all wisdom, and I will teach and admonish my fellow believers in psalms and hymns and spiritual songs with grace in my heart to the Lord (Col. 3:16).

I will walk in wisdom toward those who are without, redeeming the time (Col. 4:5).

I will ask God for any wisdom that I lack, and He will give it to me liberally (James 1:5).

Let me not be filled with bitter envy and strife in my heart, for this wisdom does not come from above but is earthly, sensual, and demonic (James 3:14–15).

Let me be filled with the wisdom from above, for it is pure, peaceful, gentle, willing to yield, full of mercy and good fruits, and without partiality and hypocrisy (James 3:17).

I say with a loud voice, "Worthy is the Lamb who was slain to receive power, riches, wisdom, strength, honor, glory, and blessing" (Rev. 5:12).

CHAPTER 2

EXERCISING FAITH FOR YOUR HEALING

And He said to her, "Daughter, your faith has made you well. Go in peace, and be healed of your affliction."

—Mark 5:34

FAITH RELEASES THE healing anointing. Unbelief blocks healing. The woman with the issue of blood put a demand on the anointing with her faith. Faith is like a vacuum that draws the anointing. Jesus not only ministered with the anointing, but He also let the people know He was anointed (Luke 4:18). When they heard He was anointed, it was their responsibility to believe and receive. The people of Nazareth did not believe and could not draw from His anointing. (See Mark 6:1–6.) He could do no mighty work in Nazareth because of their unbelief. If they would have believed, they could have drawn from His anointing and been healed.

But the woman with the issue of blood believed. She believed enough to press through the crowds, reach out, and touch the healer Himself. In Luke 8:46, Jesus says, "Somebody touched Me, for I perceived power going out from Me."

Jesus perceived that power ("virtue," KJV) had left Him. The woman drew healing power out of Him with her faith. The word *power* is the Greek word *dunamis*, which means "ability, strength, or might." When you have faith that you will be healed, you draw out the healing power of God. His power is released on your behalf. Thus, the anointing is the power of God.

> When she heard about Jesus, she came behind Him in the crowd and touched His garment.
>
> —Mark 5:27

This woman had heard of Jesus. She had heard about the healing anointing that was upon Him. She had heard that a prophet of God was ministering in Israel.

When people hear about the anointing, their faith will increase in this area, and they will then have the knowledge and faith to put a demand on the anointing. We need to know about the apostle's anointing, the prophet's anointing, the evangelist's anointing, the pastor's anointing, and the teacher's anointing. We need to know about the healing anointing and the miracle anointing. We need to know about special anointings given by the Holy Spirit.

Many in this country wonder why miracles occur so much in foreign countries. Many of the ones who attend crusades walk for miles to come to a meeting. Some travel for days. That is putting a demand on the anointing. Healing and miracles happen as a result. In America, many believers will not travel two blocks—and wonder why they don't receive miracles.

> And believers were increasingly added to the Lord, multitudes of both men and women, so that they brought the sick out into the streets and laid them on beds and couches, that at least the shadow of Peter passing by might fall on some of them. Also a multitude gathered from the surrounding cities to Jerusalem, bringing sick people and those who were tormented by unclean spirits, and they were all healed.
>
> —Acts 5:14–16

Here we see people coming "from the surrounding cities to Jerusalem." Where there is a demand, there is a supply. There was enough anointing available to heal *everyone*. These people put a demand on the anointing that flowed from the apostles. When people come to meetings, sometimes from long distances, and put a demand on the gift, they will receive miracles.

> Now it happened on a certain day, as He was teaching, that there were Pharisees and teachers of the law sitting by, who had come out of every town of Galilee, Judea, and Jerusalem. And the power of the Lord was present to heal them.
>
> —Luke 5:17

The word *power* here is *dunamis*, which is the same word translated as *virtue* in Luke 8:46 (KJV). The woman with the issue of blood drew virtue from the body of Jesus with her faith. So we can say that healing virtue was in the house as Jesus taught. When healing virtue (anointing) is present, we can use our faith to put a demand on that anointing. It will then be released for healing.

> Then behold, men brought on a bed a man who was paralyzed, whom they sought to bring in and lay before Him. And when they could not find how they might bring him in, because of the crowd, they went up on the housetop and let him down with his bed through the tiling into the midst before Jesus. When He saw their faith, He said to him, "Man, your sins are forgiven you."
>
> —Luke 5:18–20

Through their faith, they put a demand on the anointing present in that room. As a result, healing virtue was released and the man was healed. There are times when the presence of the Lord is thick like a cloud in a service. When the anointing is present to this degree, all we need to do is use our faith to put a demand upon it. Healing and miracles come as a result of putting a demand on the anointing.

We put a demand on the anointing with our *faith*. The Lord has given us the gift of faith for this purpose. The Lord desires that we use our faith to put a demand (withdrawal) on the gifts of God. Many never use their faith for this purpose.

Congregations that are built up in faith will have a tool they can use to receive from the gifts of God. Faith is a channel through which the anointing flows. Faith is like a light switch that starts the electricity flow. It is like the starter on a car that ignites the power that turns the engine. Faith is the spark that ignites the explosive power of God. It ignites the power gifts of faith, healing, and miracles.

Faith ignites the revelation gifts of word of wisdom, word of knowledge, and discerning of spirits. It ignites the utterance gifts of tongues, interpretation, and prophecy. Faith releases the ministry gifts of apostles, prophets, evangelists, pastors, and teachers.

Faith comes by hearing. The more people hear about the gifts of God, the more faith they will receive to draw from them. I teach on different operations and administrations of the Spirit.

As a pastor, I release people with different anointings and administrations to minister to the people. I teach people concerning these gifts and release them to use their faith to put a demand on these gifts.

It is amazing how profoundly ministers are able to minister in the atmosphere that is created through teaching and releasing. The people use their faith to pull the anointing right out of them, and the flow becomes so great, we have to purposely shut it off until the next service.

DECLARATIONS TO RELEASE FAITH FOR HEALING, PROSPERITY, AND DELIVERANCE

Because of Christ, I am free. Whom the Son sets free is free indeed (John 8:36).

I do not put my trust in man. I do not put my trust in flesh. I put my trust in God (Ps. 56:4).

I live by faith. I walk by faith and not by sight (2 Cor. 5:7).

I am responsible for my decisions and my choices. I make a decision. I choose life. I choose blessings. I choose the Word of God. I choose wisdom.

I thank You, Lord, that I am responsible for making my own way prosperous and having good success.

I have faith to speak to mountains, and they will obey me (Mark 11:23).

My heart will never depart from You. I will always serve God.

Thank You, Lord, for prosperity. I will flourish because I live in the days of the Messiah.

I will have prosperity, and I will have good success because of God's grace in Jesus's name.

INCREASING FAITH FOR YOUR HEALING

I declare that I, like Enoch, have a testimony that I please God through my faith (Heb. 11:5).

Because of my faith, I am pleasing to God, and He will reward me because I seek after Him diligently (Heb. 11:6).

By faith, I will sojourn in the land of promise, as in a strange country, dwelling in tabernacles with Isaac and Jacob, as I am an heir of the same promise (Heb. 11:9).

I will forsake any bondage that seeks to entrap me, looking forward by faith and setting my eyes on Him who is invisible (Heb. 11:27).

I decree and declare that by faith I will walk through my trials on dry ground, and my enemies will be drowned (Heb. 11:29).

I will encircle the immovable walls in my life, and by my faith those walls will fall down (Heb. 11:30).

Like Rahab, I will receive the men of God with peace. I will not perish with those who do not believe (Heb. 11:31).

I will subdue kingdoms, rain down righteousness, obtain promises, and stop the mouths of lions because of my faith (Heb. 11:33).

I declare that I will not only receive a good testimony of faithfulness, but I will also receive all that God has promised (Heb. 11:39–40).

I am established and anointed by God (2 Cor. 1:21).

I activate my mustard seed of faith and say to this mountain of sickness and disease in my life, "Be removed and go to another place." Nothing will be impossible to me (Matt. 17:20).

Because You have anointed me, I have faith and do not doubt that I can speak to any illness, curse it at the root, and cause it to dry up and die, just as You did to the fig tree. I also know that if I tell to this mountain of sickness that is in my way to move and be cast into the sea, it shall be done (Matt. 21:21).

I declare that I have uncommon, great faith in the power of Jesus Christ, faith that cannot be found anywhere else (Matt. 8:10).

Just as Jesus stood in the boat and spoke to the storm, I too can stand in the midst of the storms in my life and rebuke the winds and the waves to command calmness in my life. My faith overrides all my fears (Matt. 8:26).

I will not sink into faithlessness and doubt; I will be upheld by the mighty hand of God (Matt. 14:31).

I pray as Your anointed disciples prayed, "Increase my faith!" (Luke 17:5).

I will not be weak in faith. Like Abraham, I declare that my body is not dead but alive to birth out the gifts and anointing God has set aside for me (Rom. 4:19).

I will not stagger at the promise of God through unbelief, but I will stand strong in the faith, giving glory to God (Rom. 4:20).

My faith increases the more I hear, and hear by the Word of God (Rom. 10:17).

Even though I go through many common trials in this life, God, I declare that You are faithful. You will not allow me to face things beyond what I can stand. You have ordered a way of escape for me, and through Your strength I can bear it (1 Cor. 10:13).

I walk by faith and not by sight (2 Cor. 5:7).

I declare that I feel the substance and see the evidence of the things that I have faith for (Heb. 11:1).

You are Lord of all, and the worlds were framed by Your very words. You spoke into existence unseen things (Heb. 11:3).

I see through the eyes of faith the promise of things afar off. I am persuaded of their reality. I embrace them, knowing that I am a stranger and pilgrim on this earth (Heb. 11:13).

I will stand firm and not waver. I will come boldly before God, asking in faith (James 1:6).

RELEASING LIFE AND WHOLENESS INTO YOUR HEALTH

You have granted me life and favor, and Your care has preserved my spirit (Job 10:12).

My life is brighter than the noonday. Though I was in darkness, I am like the morning (Job 11:17).

My life and breath are in Your hands (Job 12:10).

The Spirit of God has made me, and the Almighty gives me life (Job 33:4).

You keep my life from perishing (Job 33:18).

You will show me the path of life (Ps. 16:11).

You meet me with blessings of goodness. You set a crown of pure gold upon my head. I asked You for my life, and You gave it to me. You gave me length of days forever and ever (Ps. 21:3–4).

Goodness and mercy follow me all the days of my life, and I will dwell in the house of the Lord forever (Ps. 23:6).

The Lord is the strength of my life (Ps. 27:1).

Your favor is for my life (Ps. 30:5).

I desire life and love many days that I may see good. Therefore, I will fear the Lord and keep my tongue from evil and my lips from speaking deceit. I will depart from evil and do good; seek peace and pursue it (Ps. 34:11–14).

Let my enemy, who seeks after my life, be put to shame and brought to dishonor (Ps. 35:4).

Rescue me from destruction and my life from the lions (Ps. 35:17)

You, O Lord, are my fountain of life (Ps. 36:9).

Let the enemy, who seeks to destroy my life, be ashamed and brought to mutual confusion. Let him be driven backward and brought to dishonor (Ps. 40:14).

You will prolong my life and make my years as many generations. I will abide before God forever. Mercy and truth will preserve me (Ps. 61:6–7).

Your loving-kindness is better than life, and my lips will praise You. I will bless You while I live. I will lift up my hands in Your name (Ps. 63:3–4).

My life is preserved from fear of the enemy (Ps. 64:1).

Preserve my life, for I am holy and You are my God. Save me because I trust in You (Ps. 86:2).

I call and You answer me. You are with me in trouble. You will deliver me and honor me. You will satisfy me with long life and show me Your salvation (Ps. 91:15–16).

I will bless the Lord and will not forget His benefits. He has forgiven my sins and healed all my diseases. He has redeemed my life from destruction and crowned me with loving-kindness and tender mercies. God has satisfied me with good things, so that my youth is renewed like the eagle's (Ps. 103:1–5).

I hope in the word You have spoken to me. It is a comfort in my affliction. Your word has given me life (Ps. 119:49–50).

I will not perish in my affliction because I delight in Your law. I will not forget Your precepts, for by them You have given me life (Ps. 119:92–93).

You will restore me and make me live (Isa. 38:16).

You have set before me the way of life and the way of death. I will follow Your way, and I shall live. My life will be my prize (Jer. 21:8–9).

You have given my life to me as a prize in all places, wherever I go (Jer. 45:5).

You have redeemed my life (Lam. 3:58).

You saw me polluted in my own blood and spoke to me and said, "Live!" (Ezek. 16:6).

I will surely live and not die because I walk in the statutes of life without committing iniquity (Ezek. 33:15).

You have brought my life up from the pit (Jon. 2:6).

Your covenant with me is one of life and peace (Mal. 2:5).

I will drink of the water You give me so that I will never thirst again. The water You give me will become in me a fountain of water springing up into everlasting life (John 4:13–14).

I have everlasting life because I have heard Your word and I believe in You. I have passed from death to life (John 5:24).

Jesus, You are the Bread of Life (John 6:48).

I will live forever because I eat of living bread (John 6:51–52).

The Spirit gives me life. His words are spirit and life to me (John 6:63).

Through You, I have life and life more abundantly (John 10:10).

I have eternal life and will not perish. I will not be snatched out of the hand of God (John 10:28–29).

I will live because I believe in Christ Jesus, who is the resurrection and the life (John 11:25–26).

You are the way, the truth, and the life (John 14:6).

I take heart because there will be no loss of life for me (Acts 27:22).

You give life to the dead and call those things that are not as though they are (Rom. 4:17).

Just as Christ was raised from the dead, I walk in the newness of life (Rom. 6:4–5).

The gift of God is eternal life in Christ Jesus my Lord (Rom. 6:23).

I am spiritually minded; therefore I have life and peace (Rom. 8:6).

The Spirit of God, who raised Jesus from the dead, dwells in me. He gives life to my mortal body through His Spirit that dwells in me (Rom. 8:11).

I am the aroma of life leading to life (2 Cor. 2:16).

The Spirit gives me life (2 Cor. 3:6).

The life of Jesus is manifested in my body. Life works in me (2 Cor. 4:10–13).

Christ lives in me. The life I now live I live by faith in the Son of God, who loves me and gave His life for me (Gal. 2:20–21).

I sow to the Spirit, and of the Spirit I reap everlasting life (Gal. 6:8).

My life is hidden with Christ in God (Col. 3:3).

I have a promise of life now and a life that is to come (1 Tim. 4:8).

My Savior, Jesus Christ, has abolished death and brought life and immortality to light through the gospel (2 Tim. 1:10–11).

I have endured temptation; therefore, I am blessed. I am approved and receive a crown of life, which the Lord has promised to those who love Him (James 1:12).

Your divine power has given to me all things that pertain to life and godliness (2 Pet. 1:3).

I have passed from death to life because I love my brothers (1 John 3:14).

I have life because I have the Son (1 John 5:12).

The breath of life from God has entered me (Rev. 11:11)

I freely receive from the fountain of life (Rev. 21:6–7).

I have a right to the tree of life because I do Your commandments (Rev. 22:14).

I take of the water of life freely (Rev. 22:17).

CHAPTER 3

HONORING THOSE WHO COME TO HEAL

> He that receiveth a prophet in the name of a prophet shall receive a prophet's reward; and he that receiveth a righteous man in the name of a righteous man shall receive a righteous man's reward.
>
> —Matthew 10:41, KJV

HONOR MEANS "VALUE, esteem, precious." To honor a man or woman of God means to value and to esteem them. We must recognize that the anointing is a precious thing. It is priceless. You cannot buy the anointing. It is given by the grace of God. *We must learn to honor ministry gifts.* When you dishonor ministry gifts, you will not be blessed by the anointing that is in them. In other words, if you do not honor the gift of healing, you will not be healed.

> Assuredly, I say to you, no prophet is accepted in his own country. But I tell you truly, many widows were in Israel in the days of Elijah, when the heaven was shut up three years and six months, and there was a great famine throughout all the land; but to

none of them was Elijah sent except to Zarephath, in the region of Sidon, to a woman who was a widow. And many lepers were in Israel in the time of Elisha the prophet, and none of them was cleansed except Naaman the Syrian.

—Luke 4:24–27

Elijah and Elisha, two anointed men of God, were in the midst of Israel for years. There were many widows who could have received a miracle through Elijah, but only one did, and she was a Gentile. No other widow put a demand on his anointing. Every leper in Israel could have been healed through Elisha, but no other leper put a demand on his anointing but Naaman. Both Elijah and Elisha had miracle and healing anointings. Those miracles and healings were available to God's people. They were walking reservoirs of the anointing. But no one cast their bucket in to draw from the pool of the anointing. No one used their faith to receive from these men of God except one Gentile woman and Naaman the Syrian.

Jesus said these men were not accepted in their own country. In other words, these men were not *valued* or *esteemed* by Israel. Their ministries were rejected and despised. As a result, many widows perished during the famine, and many lepers died of leprosy. This was not the will of the Lord. It was the will of the Lord for them to receive healing and deliverance.

This kind of rejection was not uncommon to Jesus. As we have mentioned in previous chapters, Jesus was not honored in His own hometown.

Then He went out from there and came to His own country, and His disciples followed Him. And when the Sabbath had come, He began to teach in the synagogue. And many hearing Him were astonished, saying, "Where did this Man get these things? And what wisdom is this which is given to Him, that such mighty works are performed by His hands! Is this not the carpenter, the Son of Mary, and brother of James, Joses, Judas, and Simon? And are not His sisters here with us?" And they were offended at Him. But Jesus said to them, "*A prophet is not without honor except in his own country, among his own relatives, and in his own house.*" Now He could do no mighty work there, except that He laid His hands on a few sick people and healed them. And He marveled because of their unbelief.

—Mark 6:1–6, emphasis added

Giving honor to the man of God who is coming to minister is another level of faith in the indwelling power of the Holy Spirit working in us. If you can't show honor, respect, and acceptance to the man of God, you are basically saying, "I don't believe the Holy Spirit is working in you, and I do not receive what you have come to give." You are essentially refusing your healing.

Giving Double Honor

Let the elders that rule well be counted worthy of double honour, especially they who labour in the word and doctrine. For the scripture saith, Thou shalt not muzzle the ox that treadeth out the corn. And, The labourer is worthy of his reward.

—1 Timothy 5:17–18, KJV

Remember, the word *honor* means "value." How much do you value the ministers that God has placed in your midst? Paul is talking here about supporting the ministry. In this case, to *honor* means "to give to and support financially." Congregations who do not bless their ministers financially are dishonoring them. You cannot receive from their anointing if you do not honor them in this way. You will receive more from the anointing, within the men and women of God, if you honor them with your giving.

In Acts 28, the people's giving followed the miraculous healing, but there was unmistakable honor given once they recognized the healing power activated in Paul.

> But when Paul had gathered a bundle of sticks and laid them on the fire, a viper came out because of the heat, and fastened on his hand. So when the natives saw the creature hanging from his hand, they said to one another, "No doubt this man is a murderer, whom, though he has escaped the sea, yet justice does not allow to live." But he shook off the creature into the fire and suffered no harm.
>
> —Acts 28:3–5

The men watch Paul for a while longer to see if he would swell up or fall out and die. When neither of these things happened, they were amazed and thought the power he demonstrated was godlike. Not only this, but the leader of this island, Publius, also treated Paul and his companions with great respect and honor. He entertained them and received them courteously for three days. Therefore, there was no hindrance when Publius's father needed to be healed of dysentery. Then the healing just began to trickle down to everyone who was sick on the island.

The giving of honor flowed from the top. The leader of this island knew how to treat guests. He honored them first, and the healings began to flow. But it didn't stop there. The people show additional honor, or double honor, by making sure they lacked nothing for their departure.

> So when this was done, the rest of those on the island who had diseases also came and were healed. They also honored us in many ways; and when we departed, they provided such things as were necessary.
>
> —Acts 28:9–10

It is not hard to see the correlation between giving honor and receiving healing. A gift is given best when it is well received. How much better does a singer or actor perform when their gift is appreciated by the audience? This is why so many Israelites died during the famine. They simply did not appreciate the gifts of Elijah and Elisha.

> And Elisha died, and they buried him. And the bands of the Moabites invaded the land at the coming in of the year. And it came to pass, as they were burying a man, that, behold, they spied a band of men; and they cast the man into the sepulcher of Elisha: and

when the man was let down, and touched the bones
of Elisha, he revived, and stood up on his feet.

—2 Kings 13:20–21, KJV

Elisha had enough anointing in *his bones* to raise a man from
the dead. Imagine the anointing that was available to Israel while
he was alive! Because they did not honor, respect, or receive his
gifts, they did not receive the miracles they needed. Every leper
in Israel needed a miracle. The Lord, in His mercy, saw the need
and provided the man of God with His anointing. It was up to
Israel to put a demand on it. Their needs were not met because
there was no demand. There was no faith. There was no honor.
If they would have honored the prophet of God, they would have
been healed. The anointing was available. It was strong enough.
But there was no demand. As stated earlier, *where there is no
demand, there is no supply.*

RELEASING HONOR TO THE MAN OF GOD

Let my life be precious in the sight of the man of God so that I
will be preserved (2 Kings 1:13–14).

I declare that the man of God in this city is honorable, and
all that he says comes to pass. He will show us the way to go.
When I go to him for direction, I will bless him with valuable
gifts (1 Sam. 9:6–9).

The man of God will pray for me and I will be restored. I will make room in my home for him so that he can be refreshed (1 Kings 13:6–8).

The word of the Lord is in the mouth of the man of God (1 Kings 17:24).

The man of God pursues righteousness, godliness, faith, love, patience, and gentleness. He fights the good fight of faith and lays hold of eternal life (1 Tim. 6:11–13).

The man of God is complete and thoroughly equipped for every good work (2 Tim. 3:17).

I will go everywhere to borrow vessels to accommodate the endless flow of anointing that the man of God has spoken into my household. This anointing will bring prosperity to my children and me (2 Kings 4:1–7).

I will follow the instructions that the man of God gives me, so that my flesh will be restored like that of a little child, and I will be clean (2 Kings 5:14).

The man of God is anointed to minister to the Lord as priest over His people throughout the generations (Exod. 40:15).

The man of God, who is consecrated to minister as priest, will seek God in prayer on my behalf (Lev. 16:32–33).

The Lord will exhalt the horn of His anointed; He will give strength to the man of God (1 Sam. 2:10).

The man of God will be raised up and will do according to what is in the heart and mind of God. God will build him a sure house, and he will walk before God's anointed forever (1 Sam. 2:35).

God forbid that I do anything out of line to the Lord's anointed. I will not stretch my hand out against him, seeing that he is anointed of the Lord (1 Sam. 24:6).

I will not stretch my hand out against the man of God, for he is the Lord's anointed (1 Sam. 24:10–11).

I will not touch the Lord's anointed, and I will do His prophets no harm (1 Chron. 16:22).

Lord God, do not turn away the face of Your anointed; remember the mercies of the man of God (2 Chron. 6:42).

The Lord saves His anointed; He will answer him from His holy heaven with the saving strength of His right hand (Ps. 20:6).

The Lord strengthens the man of God. His is his saving refuge (Ps. 28:8).

God has anointed the man of God with the oil of gladness more than any of his companions (Ps. 45:7).

The Lord has found the man of God. With His holy oil, He has anointed him. With the hand of God, he shall be established. The arm of the Lord will strengthen him. His enemies will not outwit him, neither will the son of wickedness afflict him. The Lord will beat down his foes before his face (Ps. 89:20–23).

The Spirit of the Lord God is upon the man of God, because the Lord has anointed him to preach good tidings to the poor. He has sent him to heal the brokenhearted; to proclaim liberty to the captives and the opening of the prison to those who are bound; to proclaim the acceptable year of the Lord and the day of vengeance of our God; to comfort all who mourn; to console those who mourn in Zion; to give them beauty for ashes, the oil of joy for mourning, and the garment of praise for the spirit of heaviness, that we may be called trees of righteousness, the planting of the Lord, that He may be glorified (Isa. 61:1–3).

God has anointed the man of God with the Holy Spirit and with power. He will go about doing good and healing all who are oppressed by the devil, because God is with him (Acts 10:38–39).

The man of God is established with me in Christ. He has been anointed by God. He is sealed by God and has been given the Holy Spirit in his heart as a guarantee (2 Cor. 1:21–22).

I will rise before the gray headed and honor the presence of an old man (Lev. 19:32).

The man of God honors the Lord; therefore, he will be honored (1 Sam. 2:30).

The man of God will sit in the place of honor among those who are invited (1 Sam. 9:22).

God has crowned the man of God with glory and honor (Ps. 8:5).

The Lord has given the man of God his heart's desire and has not withheld the request of his lips. The Lord has met him with the blessings of goodness and set a crown of pure gold upon his head. He asked God for life, and He gave it to him (Ps. 21:2–4).

The man of God will call upon the Lord, and He will answer him. God will be with him in trouble. He will deliver him and honor him (Ps. 91:15).

Wisdom brings him honor when he embraces her (Prov. 4:8).

The man of God follows righteousness and mercy. He finds life, righteousness, and honor (Prov. 21:21).

The man of God is humble and fears the Lord. He is given riches, honor, and life (Prov. 22:4).

The man of God is humble in spirit; he retains honor (Prov. 29:23).

The man of God will have double honor instead of shame. He will rejoice in his portion instead of being confused. In his land, he will possess double. Everlasting joy will be his (Isa. 61:7).

The man of God honors his Father in heaven. He does not seek his own glory (John 8:49).

Glory, honor, and peace go to the man of God because he works what is good (Rom. 2:10).

Let the elders who rule well be counted worthy of double honor (1 Tim. 5:17).

Chapter 4

Touching the Hem

For she said within herself, If I may but touch his garment, I shall be whole.

—Matthew 9:21, KJV

THE ROTHERHAM TRANSLATION says, "If only I touch his mantle." The *mantle* represents the *anointing*. Elisha took up the mantle that fell from Elijah (2 Kings 2:13). He smote the waters with Elijah's mantle. When God called Elisha, He used Elijah to cast His mantle upon him (1 Kings 19:19). This represented the anointing coming upon him to stand in the office of a prophet. We call this the *prophetic mantle*.

Jesus walked and ministered as a prophet of God. He ministered under a prophetic mantle. This mantle also included healing and miracles. The woman with the issue of blood pressed through the crowd to touch His mantle. She was putting a demand upon His prophetic mantle. As a result, she received a miracle. There are different mantles given to different people. As you touch the mantle of a particular office, you will draw virtue and power from that anointing. I am not referring to touching a person physically but drawing from them *spiritually*. Faith is the channel through which you draw. It is the pipeline.

> And when the men of that place had knowledge of
> him, they sent out into all that country round about,
> and brought unto him all that were diseased; and
> besought him that they might only touch the hem
> of his garment: and as many as touched were made
> perfectly whole.
>
> —Matthew 14:35–36, KJV

The Montgomery translation says they "kept begging him." Have you ever had someone continue to beg you? They are demanding something of you. This is how you put a demand on the anointing. To *beseech* means "to beg for urgently or anxiously, to request earnestly, to implore, to make supplication." It means to *seek*. It is the laying aside of pride. You admit you have a need and beseech someone who has the ability to help you. If you never recognize your need for and utter dependence upon the anointing, you will never put a demand on it.

> And whithersoever he entered, into villages, or cities,
> or country, they laid the sick in the streets, and
> besought him that they might touch if it were but the
> border of his garment: and as many as touched him
> were made whole.
>
> —Mark 6:56, KJV

Everywhere Jesus went people were putting a demand on the anointing. They besought Him to touch His garment. They drew the healing and miracles out of Him. You may say this happened in every city because it was a sovereign move of God. You may think the people had nothing to do with it. But remember, it didn't happen in His hometown of Nazareth. They did not beseech to touch Him in Nazareth. These miracles didn't occur in Nazareth because the people didn't put a demand on the anointing. In other villages and cities, they did, and they were made whole.

If you want to be healed you need to reach out and touch the hem of Jesus's garment. You need to beseech the anointing that He has left on the men and women of God in your life. Pull on their anointings, and demand your healing miracle. Let them pray for you and lay hands on you so that you can be healed.

As I mentioned in the introduction, healing can be transferrable through the anointed cloths or clothes coming from the man or woman of God. The healing anointing is tangible. We used anointed and prayed-over cloths to give to people at my church. We have received many testimonies of healing resulting from this. Paul confirms this phenomenon in Acts 19:11–13. By touching the handkerchiefs and aprons from Paul's body, sick people received miraculous healings. The Bible says that the diseases left these people and demons went out of them. This requires a very high level of faith and an increased demand on the gifts of God's anointed ones. You cannot hesitate to have high expectancy to receive healing by touching a garment. Just like the woman with the issue of blood had, you must *draw* from that touch.

GETTING CLOSE TO THE HEALER
THROUGH HIS WORD

And it came to pass, that, as the people pressed upon him to hear the word of God, he stood by the lake of

Gennesaret... And he entered into one of the ships, which was Simon's, and prayed him that he would thrust out a little from the land. And he sat down, and taught the people out of the ship.

—Luke 5:1, 3, KJV

Faith comes by hearing (Rom. 10:17). That is why we need to *hear* about the healing anointing. We need teaching concerning that anointing. To put a demand on the teaching gift, you must have a desire for knowledge. The New English translation says the people crowded upon Him to listen to the Word of God. These people were putting a demand upon His teaching gift. There was such a demand that He needed to borrow Simon's ship to teach the crowds. How often do people crowd into buildings to hear teaching? Only those who are hungry for the Word will press to hear. Their hunger for the things of God will cause them to put a demand on the gifts of God.

Jesus always responded to people who put a demand on Him through their hunger for the things of God. He never turned them away empty. As I travel, ministering the Word of God, I discern different levels of spiritual hunger in different areas. Some people will press to hear the Word. They will draw the revelation right out of you. You will teach in a higher level of anointing because of the hunger of the people.

I don't want to teach people who are not hungry for the Word. In some places, people will just sit there and look at you. They really don't want anything from God. There is no hunger, no press. If they had to come early to get a seat, you would not see them. The spiritual principle we are sharing in this book is what

I call the *law of supply and demand*. Where there is no demand, there is no supply. Apathetic, passive Christians don't receive much from the gifts of God.

> On the next Sabbath almost the whole city came together to hear the word of God.
>
> —Acts 13:44

Not only can individuals put a demand on the anointing, but entire cities can as well.

This verse excites me because of the possibility of entire cities desiring to hear the Word of God. I believe in these last days the Lord will cause a hunger in cities to hear the Word. When ministry gifts come into the city, people will gather and put a demand on those gifts. This has happened somewhat in the past, but it will happen to an even greater extent in these days, as the Lord pours out His Spirit upon all flesh.

As Paul and Barnabas ministered in Antioch of Pisidia, the Gentiles were the ones who put a demand on their apostolic gifts. The Jews were beginning to harden their hearts. They did not desire to hear the good news of salvation. Paul and Barnabas began to turn to the Gentiles. Ministry gifts will always be wherever the demand is. The Gentiles were the ones who were hungry. The gifts of God were released on their behalf. As a result, they received salvation, healing, and deliverance.

> And the word of the Lord was published throughout all the region.
>
> —Acts 13:49, KJV

As exciting as cities coming together to hear the Word may seem, it is even more exciting for *regions* to be charged by the power of God! Because there was a hunger in the city, and the gifts of God were released as a result, the entire *region* was affected. Mass healings will take place across large geographic areas. I am not satisfied with only my city being taken for God, but I want to affect my region! When there is a hunger for the Word of God in a city, it will affect the entire region, and the anointing for teaching, miracles, and healing can be released. Once a demand is put on the anointing, that anointing will be released on behalf of entire cities and regions.

PRAYERS THAT BRING HEALING BY TOUCH

The Lord will deliver me in six troubles, and in seven, no evil will touch me (Job 5:19).

I am confident deep within myself that if I will but touch the hem of Your garment, I will be made whole (Matt. 9:21).

As the knowledge of who You are spreads, people will send out for the sick and diseased in all the surrounding regions so that they too can touch the hem of Your garment (Matt. 14:35–36).

I press in to touch You, Jesus, and You will heal me of my plague (Mark 3:10).

I will reach for Your clothes and touch them, and I shall be made whole (Mark 5:28).

As Your Spirit goes forth in the villages, cities, and countries, the sick will be laid before You. They will beg to touch even the border of Your garment, and as they touch You, they will be made whole (Mark 6:56).

The blind will come before You, begging to touch You. You will touch them and their sight will be restored. They will see things clearly (Mark 8:22–25).

Multitudes will seek to touch You, and virtue will be transferred out of You, and all of them will be healed (Luke 6:19).

Just like Elisha, even the bones of the man or woman of God You have anointed will be filled with life and healing so much so that, by their touch, the dead will be revived and stand up on their feet (2 Kings 13:21).

Let Your seraphims fly unto me, and touch me with a live coal from Your altar so that all my sin, sickness, and iniquity be taken away (Isa. 6:6–7).

Lord, put forth Your hand to touch me. Put Your life-giving and healing words in my mouth (Jer. 1:9).

You have sent Your angels, and they touched me and strengthened me (Dan. 10:18).

You have put forth Your hand and touched me. I know that I am immediately made clean (Matt. 8:2–3).

The man of God has touched me. My sickness has left me. Now I can arise and minister to those around me (Matt. 8:15).

You touched my eyes, O Lord, and according to my faith, they have been opened (Matt. 9:29–30).

You came and touched me. I will arise and not be afraid. I will lift up my eyes to see no man except Jesus (Matt. 17:7–8).

You had compassion on me and touched my eyes. Immediately I received my sight, and I will follow You (Matt. 20:34).

You took me aside from the multitude and touched my ears and my tongue. And straightway, my ears have been opened and my tongue has been loosed (Mark 7:33–35).

You will come and touch my lifeless body. You have commanded me to arise. Immediately, I will sit up and begin to speak (Luke 7:14–15).

Yes, I have suffered this far, but You will touch my ears and will heal me (Luke 22:51).

Everyone You lay Your hands on is healed (Luke 4:40).

Lay Your hands on the sick and heal them (Mark 6:5).

You lay Your hands on the sick and deformed and immediately they are made straight, and they will glorify God (Luke 13:13).

Like the apostle Paul, may the man of God come and lay hands on me and heal me (Acts 28:8).

PRAYING THE WORD FOR HEALING

The healing of the Lord will spring forth speedily (Isa. 58:8).

I cried out to You, God, and You healed me. You kept me alive (Ps. 30:2–3).

By Your stripes, I am healed (Isa. 53:5).

Speak a word, Lord, and heal me this very hour (Matt. 8:8, 13).

I declare that I am in good health; I am alive (Gen. 43:28).

The fear of the Lord is health to my body and strength to my bones (Prov. 3:7–8).

I will give attention to the words of God. I will incline my ear to His sayings. They will not depart from my eyes. I will keep them in the midst of my heart because they are life to me and health to my body (Prov. 4:20–22).

I will speak with wisdom and promote health (Prov. 12:18).

I will receive and speak only pleasant words. They are like a honeycomb, sweetness to my soul and health to my bones (Prov. 16:24).

I declare that I prosper in all things and am in good health, just as my soul prospers (3 John 2–3).

As heaven and Earth are my witnesses, I choose life so that both my descendents and I will live (Deut. 30:19).

I declare, O Lord, that You are my life and the length of my days. I love You. I choose to obey You. I cling to You (Deut. 30:20).

I declare, O Lord, that You are the restorer of my life and the nourisher of my old age (Ruth 4:15).

You have redeemed my life from all adversity (2 Sam. 4:9–10).

You do not take away life but devise ways so that I will be drawn in close to You (2 Sam. 14:14–15).

I offer sacrifices of sweet savor unto God and pray for my life and the lives of my children (Ezra 6:10).

If it pleases You and as I have found favor in Your sight, let my life be given to me (Esther 7:3).

I gather together with other believers and stand for my life. I destroy, slay, and cause to perish all the powers that would rise up to assault me. I take the spoil of them for prey (Esther 8:11).

CHAPTER 5

DRAWING FROM THE WELL

Jesus therefore, being wearied from His journey,
sat thus by the well. It was about the sixth hour. A
woman of Samaria came to draw water.

John 4:6–7

THE HEALING ANOINTING that accompanies the ministry gifts
is like a well. The Samaritan woman who came to the well
that day may not have appeared to have any physical issues, but
Jesus knew she needed healing. Her need to draw from the spiritual well that Jesus had within Him was being played out in the
natural by her physical need to draw water from Jacob's well.

Jesus was fully operational in the Spirit because the Word of
God dwelled in Him—He was the Word (John 1:1–2). Therefore,
His level of discernment was able to pierce through the natural
and see this woman's spiritual need. (See Hebrews 4:12.) But it
didn't stop there. It wasn't just His recognition of her need that
got her need met, but it was also about how she began to pull on
the well of anointing that Jesus had within Him. She began to
inquire, "How is it that You, being a Jew, ask a drink from me, a
Samaritan woman?...Sir, You have nothing to draw with, and the
well is deep. Where then do You get that living water? Are You

greater than our father Jacob, who gave us the well, and drank from it himself, as well as his sons and his livestock?" (John 4:9, 11–12). The more she pressed in and the more she surrendered to the longing for wholeness in her heart, the deeper she dug into the well of the Spirit. At one point she just came right out and demanded, "Sir, give me this water, that I may not thirst, nor come here to draw" (v. 15).

This woman put a demand on the Spirit that will never be refused. The Bible says in Revelation 21:6 that God will freely give the water of the fountain of life to anyone who thirsts. (See also Revelation 22:17.) Are you thirsty for healing? Will you dig deep into the well of the Spirit for your healing?

Just like this woman, you can put a demand upon the healing anointing and draw from it. There is a never-ending supply of the Spirit available to every believer.

> For I know that this shall turn to my salvation through your prayer, and the supply of the Spirit of Jesus Christ.
>
> —Philippians 1:19, KJV

When I look at ministry gifts of the Spirit, I see a *living reservoir*—or *well*. In that well is a supply of the anointing. The Lord has deposited His anointing in individuals for the perfecting of the saints. It is our responsibility to draw from that supply. Just like Jesus at the well, men and women of God have been empowered through the Holy Spirit with miracles, revelation, and deliverance for you in the well. If you put a demand on the anointing in that well, miracles will flow out of them to you.

> And the whole multitude sought to touch him: for there went virtue out of him, and healed them all.
> —Luke 6:19, KJV

These people were putting a demand on the anointing. Virtue came out of Jesus because the people drew from the well of His anointing. They drew it out by seeking to touch Him. You can literally pull the anointing out of ministry gifts by your faith, by fasting and prayer, by worshiping in Spirit and in truth, by walking in obedience to the Word of God, by staying in the presence of God, and by honoring the man or woman of God. If these people would have just sat back and waited for Jesus to put it on them, they probably would not have received anything. Many times believers just sit back and wait for the man or woman of God to do something. He has placed the well in our midst, and we have to draw from it.

SUPPLY AND DEMAND

The Lord spoke to my heart the fact that there is always a supply when there is a demand. The drug problems in our cities would not exist if there were no demand for drugs. Because there is a demand for drugs, there is a supply. It is the same with the anointing. If there is no demand, there will be no supply. Hungry saints who put a demand on ministry gifts will always have a supply of the anointing. I have ministered in churches where there was such a hunger and thirst for the anointing until they literally pulled the power right out of me. I have ministered in other places where there was no demand, and as a result nothing happened. The people just sat back and waited for something to happen, and nothing did. There was no hunger or expectancy for revelation, utterances, or miracles.

As a pastor, I teach the members of our local assembly to draw from the ministry gifts that minister in our services. I tell them to put a demand on the anointing in the apostles, prophets, evangelists, pastors, and teachers. I teach them that these gifts from God have a supply in them, and it is their responsibility to draw from that supply.

Many ministers who have ministered at our local church are shocked by the anointing in which they flow. This happens because I teach the people to pull it out of them. Ministers love to minister in that type of atmosphere. The flow is much easier because the people are pulling *from* you instead of blocking you.

> And behold, two blind men sitting by the road, when they heard that Jesus was passing by, cried out, saying, "Have mercy on us, O Lord, Son of David!" Then the multitude warned them that they should be quiet; but they cried out all the more, saying, "Have mercy on us, O Lord, Son of David!"
>
> —Matthew 20:30–31

These men put a *demand* on Jesus. They cried out even when the multitude was rebuking them, telling them to be silent. They had to press past the opposition of the crowd to receive their miracle. If they had remained silent, they would not have received a miracle. They had to put a demand on the anointing. Jesus was passing by. If they did not put a demand on His anointing, He would have passed *them* by. It is like drawing money from a bank. You must go to the teller with a withdrawal slip and make a demand on the account. That is why they are called demand deposit accounts, or DDAs. If you never make a demand on the account, you will never withdraw anything from the account. A church should never allow a ministry gift to come in their midst and minister without putting a demand on the anointing.

> Then He went out from there and came to His own country, and His disciples followed Him. And when the Sabbath had come, He began to teach in the synagogue. And many hearing Him were astonished, saying, "Where did this Man get these things? And what wisdom is this which is given to Him, that such mighty works are performed by His hands! Is this not the carpenter, the Son of Mary, and brother of James, Joses, Judas, and Simon? And are not His sisters here with us?" And they were offended at Him. But Jesus said to them, "A prophet is not without honor except in his own country, among his own relatives, and in his own house." Now He could do no mighty work there, except that He laid His hands on a few sick people and healed them. And He marveled because of their unbelief. Then He went about the villages in a circuit, teaching.
>
> —Mark 6:1–6

There, right in their midst, was a supply—*a well of the anointing.* In that well was salvation, healing, deliverance, and miracles. Jesus was a walking well of anointing. They had the chance to put a demand on it and draw from it, but they did not because of *unbelief.* They did not see Him as a well of the anointing but as a carpenter, "the Son of Mary, and brother of James, Joses, Judas, and Simon." They looked at Him and judged Him in the natural. However, if they had looked at Him in the spirit, they would have seen Him as a well or a reservoir of the anointing. They would have drawn out of Him miracles and healing *by faith.*

We must begin to view ministry gifts in the spirit. You must see your pastor as a walking well of the anointing. You must put a demand upon the anointing and draw the miracles out of Him. There is nothing wrong with ministers telling people what they are anointed for. If you have a healing anointing, tell the people. Give them a chance to draw from that well of anointing. If you have a prophetic anointing, tell the people. Let them draw the prophetic words out of you. If you have a teaching anointing, tell the people. Let them draw the knowledge, revelation, and healing out of you.

DRAW FROM ANOINTED VESSELS

And there were set there six waterpots of stone, after the manner of the purifying of the Jews, containing two or three firkins apiece. Jesus saith unto them, Fill the waterpots with water. And they filled them up to the brim. And he saith unto them, Draw out now, and

> bear unto the governor of the feast. And they bare it.
> When the ruler of the feast had tasted the water that
> was made wine, and knew not whence it was: (but the
> servants which drew the water knew;) the governor of
> the feast called the bridegroom, and saith unto him,
> Every man at the beginning doth set forth good wine;
> and when men have well drunk, then that which is
> worse: but thou hast kept the good wine until now.
>
> —John 2:6–10, KJV

The story of the first miracle of Jesus at Cana of Galilee is prophetic. The six water pots of stone represent the earthen vessels that the Lord uses (2 Cor. 4:7). Six is the number of man. Man was created on the sixth day. Jesus commanded the water pots be filled with water. Water represents the Word (Eph. 5:26). Servants of God need to be filled with the Word of God. Apostles, prophets, evangelists, pastors, and teachers are to be filled with the Word. The Lord will fill you with the Word so that others can draw from you.

Jesus then told them to draw out of the water pots. As they drew out, the water was turned into wine. Wine represents the Holy Spirit. It represents the anointing of God. We are to draw out of the ministry gifts. *Draw* is the Greek word *antleo*, meaning to dip water with a bucket or pitcher.

We are to use our buckets and draw out of the earthen vessels that God has filled with His Word. When I get around anointed ministry gifts, my bucket is out and I am ready to draw. When the Lord's vessels come into the local church, we are to draw from them. We draw because we have needs. We draw because we need to be healed. The mother of Jesus said to Him, "They have no wine" (John 2:3). There was a need at the marriage feast for wine. When there is a need for the anointing and flow of the Spirit, we must draw out of the earthen vessels the Lord has given us. We must use our faith to draw out the wine when there is a need.

Ministry gifts must spend time filling up on the Word. We must allow the Lord to fill our vessels up with the water of the Word. As we minister, we must allow the saints of God to draw from us. There are so many with needs. They need the wine of the Holy Ghost that will flow from us.

Truly, whether filling up or drawing from the Holy Ghost, we need the power of God flowing in our lives. You are reading this because you have a need. You need the power of God to flow healing into your life. It is my sincere hope and prayer that this revelation will cause you to draw your healing from the Spirit by way of the earthen vessels He has anointed and that you will drink from the water of life God gives so freely so that you can begin to receive in abundance the fullness of God in your life.

DRAWING HEALTH AND LIFE FROM THE WELL OF THE SPIRIT

You have opened my eyes to see the well of the water of Your Spirit. I will fill my cup and drink (Gen. 21:19).

I stand by the well of water from Your Spirit, and what I declare shall come to pass (Gen. 24:43).

I will dig deep into the well of Your Spirit, for you have made room for me and I will be fruitful in the land (Gen. 26:22).

I dig deep in the valley of my circumstances; there I will find a well of springing water (Gen. 26:19).

I will dig and dig until I find the water of Your Spirit (Gen. 26:32).

I am fruitful by the well of Your Spirit. I abide in strength, and the arms of my hands are made strong by the hands of the almighty God (Gen. 49:22–24).

My spirit encamps in Elim by the twelve wells of water and seventy palm trees, for You have healed me and none of the diseases of Egypt will come upon me (Exod. 15:26–27).

With understanding and wisdom, I draw out the counsel that You have placed in the deep well of my heart (Prov. 20:5), and I will find healing.

With joy I draw healing water out of the wells of salvation (Isa. 12:3).

I dug into the well of Your Spirit and drank Your water (Isa. 37:25).

Give me living water, O God, so that I will not thirst anymore or go to earthly wells to draw water (John 4:15).

I drink freely from the water that You have given me. It is a well of water that springs up into everlasting life (John 4:14).

I speak to the well of the Lord deep within me, "Spring up, O well!" I will dig this well according to Your direction (Num. 21:16–18).

Like David, I long to drink of the water of the well of Bethlehem (2 Sam. 23:15).

Let Your rain fall and fill the pools of the well that I have made in my spirit (Ps. 84:6).

My mouth is a well of life (Prov. 10:11). I speak life, health, and prosperity to my mind, body, and spirit.

A fountain of gardens, a well of living waters, and streams from Lebanon dwell within me (Song of Sol. 4:15).

HEALING AND BLESSING FROM THE WATER OF LIFE

I thirst; therefore, I come to You and drink living water (John 7:37).

My belly overflows with rivers of living water because I believe in You (John 7:38).

I come to You with weeping, and You lead me to walk by the rivers of water where I will not stumble (Jer. 31:9).

I am like a tree planted by the rivers of water. I bring forth fruit in my season. My leaves do not wither. Everything I do prospers (Ps. 1:3).

I am like a tree planted by the waters. My roots spread out by the waters. When the heat and drought come, my leaves will stay green and I will not cease to bear fruit (Jer. 17:8).

I have been planted in good soil and by great waters. I am a splendid vine that brings forth branches and bears fruit (Ezek. 17:8).

My mother is like a vine planted by the waters. She is fruitful and full of branches because of the abundant water (Ezek. 19:10).

You have shown me a pure river of water of life, clear as crystal, proceeding out of the throne of God and of the Lamb. In the midst of this river was the tree of life, whose leaves were for the healing of nations—and there shall be no more curse of sickness upon my life (Rev. 22:1–3).

I drink of the water of life freely (Rev. 22:17).

The Alpha and Omega, the beginning and the end, has given to me the fountain of the water of life freely, and I drink (Rev. 21:6).

I serve the Lord my God. He has blessed my bread and my water and has taken away sickness from the midst of me (Exod. 23:25).

Like Moses, I bring my family before the Lord and wash them with the water of the Word (Lev. 8:6).

I will bathe myself in the running water of the Spirit to cleanse myself of any issue—physical, spiritual, and emotional—and I shall be clean (Lev. 15:13).

I will speak to the rock of my salvation, and He shall bring forth His water so that I can drink (Num. 20:8).

I am like groves of palms, like fruitful gardens planted by the riverside, like aloes planted by the Lord, like cedars beside the waters. He will pour out His Spirit over me like gushing buckets of water, and my seed will be supplied with all they need (Num. 24:5–7).

I will be purified with the water of separation (Num. 31:23).

I am like the tree whose roots are spread out by the waters, whose branches are refreshed with the dew. New honors are constantly bestowed on me, and my strength is continually renewed (Job 29:19–20).

God draws the water up into small drops and causes it to rain on me so that I am blessed (Job 36:27–28).

As the deer pants after the water brooks, so my soul pants after You, O God (Ps. 42:1).

My soul thirsts for God, for the living God (Ps. 42:2).

My soul thirsts for God, and my flesh longs after Him in a dry and thirsty land where no water is (Ps. 63:1).

You send Your water that flows out of the abundant river of God. Your water never runs dry, and it brings forth a bountiful harvest (Ps. 65:9–10).

The Spirit of God shall come down upon me like rain upon the mowed grass, like showers that water the earth (Ps. 72:6).

You have turned the desert of my life into pools of water, and the dry ground into water springs. You make me dwell in fertile places. You bless me and multiply my seed greatly (Ps. 107:35–38).

My heart is like the rivers of water in God's hands (Prov. 21:1).

You refresh me like the rivers of water in a dry place. You shelter me like the cool shadow of a great rock (Isa. 32:2).

The dry parched ground in my life will become a pool, and the thirsty land springs of living water (Isa. 35:7).

The Lord will hear me, for I am poor in health and needy and in search of living water. He will not forsake me. He will open rivers in high places and fountains in the midst of valleys. He will make the wilderness a pool of water and the dry land springs of water (Isa. 41:17–18).

You have poured your water upon me because I was thirsty. You flooded my dry ground. You have poured Your Spirit and

Your blessing over my offspring. They will spring up like the grass and like willows by the watercourse (Isa. 44:3–4).

I will not hunger or thirst; neither shall I be overtaken by the heat of the day, because You have mercy on me and will lead me by the springs of water (Isa. 49:10).

The Lord will guide me continually and will satisfy my soul in drought. He will keep me strong and healthy. I will be like a watered garden, like an ever-flowing spring (Isa. 58:11).

You have washed me with water. You have washed off my blood and anointed me with oil (Ezek. 16:9).

You will sprinkle water on me and I will be clean from all my filthiness and idols. You will give me a new heart and spirit (Ezek. 36:25–26).

Let the rivers of Judah flow with waters and a fountain from the house of the Lord so that my valleys can be watered (Joel 3:18).

Let Your angel come and trouble the waters so that I may step in and be made whole of my disease (John 5:4).

I am sanctified and cleansed through the washing of the water by the Word. I have been presented glorious before the Lord, having no spot or wrinkle. I am holy and without blemish (Eph. 5:26–27).

I draw near to the Lord with a true heart full of faith. My heart has been sprinkled clean by the blood of the Lamb and my body washed with pure water (Heb. 10:22).

With You is the fountain of life, and in Your light I see light (Ps. 36:9).

I will heed the advice of the wise, for it is a fountain of life. By obeying, I will avoid the snares of death (Prov. 13:14).

Death will not touch me because I fear the Lord and He is my fountain of life (Prov. 14:27).

CHAPTER 6

ACTIVATING YOUR HEALING GIFT

> Wherefore I put thee in remembrance that thou stir up the gift of God, which is in thee by the putting on of my hands.
>
> —2 Timothy 1:6, KJV

MEN AND WOMEN of God, it is your responsibility to stir up the gift that God has placed in you. You have been touched, healed, and delivered; now it's time for you to give back. Jesus said, "Heal the sick, cleanse the lepers, raise the dead, cast out devils: freely ye have received, freely give" (Matt. 10:8, KJV). Don't hold back from others what you have been given. Stay in the stream of the anointing, and keep your gift stirred up so that someone else can experience a breakthrough in their situation. Don't be passive about your gift. Passivity about the healing anointing can hinder the flow.

Some of the people are too passive, too lazy to stir up the gift. They allow their gift to remain dormant, or they back up when they encounter a little resistance in the spirit. They sit back and wait for the servant of God to do everything. They don't exercise their faith to put a demand on the gift. But you don't have to do that; you can begin to press into the Spirit just as you did for your healing and receive anointing to pass that healing on to someone else. You must resist passivity in order for others to benefit fully from your gift.

Often in ministry, I will *begin* to flow in prophecy, miracles, or healing because I sense a *demand*—and there is a demand for what you have. There is nothing more that people desire and need in the innermost part of their spirits than a touch from God. The more you stay connected to the endless flow of the Spirit, the more miracles will flow out of you. And the people will begin to put a demand on what you have, and you will flow even more. It's that supply and demand cycle all over again. It is like priming the pump. Once the water begins to flow, it comes gushing out. Jesus said that out of our bellies would flow rivers of living water. All we need to do is get the flow started. It will *begin* when there is a *demand*. Once it begins, it will continue to flow until every need is met.

What Is the Anointing?

> But you have an anointing from the Holy One, and you know all things.
>
> —1 John 2:20

> But the anointing which you have received from Him abides in you.
>
> —1 John 2:27

The word *anointing* here is taken from the Greek word *charisma*. It means an unguent or smearing (represented by smearing with oil). It also means an *endowment* of the Holy Spirit. An endowment is a gift of the Holy Spirit. It is the power or ability of God. There are diversities of gifts (endowments or miraculous faculties).

To draw from the anointing is to receive from the gift or ability of God. You can receive healing, deliverance, and miracles in this way. Apostles, prophets, evangelists, pastors, and teachers have an anointing given to them from God. They have endowments or miraculous faculties given to them by grace. These endowments are given for the benefit of the saints.

God will anoint you to have healing virtue in your life, if you ask. The Bible says that we have not because we ask not (James 4:2). When you ask God for this anointing, it will be not only in your hands but also in your clothes. Don't be afraid to go boldly to the throne of grace in your time of need, and you need the anointing of God to be active in your life. You need His anointing so that wherever you encounter sick people and touch them they will get healed. In this kingdom age signs and wonders need to accompany the message of the gospel. Jesus said that whatever works He did, we will do even greater (John 14:12), as we fast and pray that healing virtue will increase in our lives. Jesus had virtue because He spent time fasting and praying. Ask God for an apostolic anointing of healing power, miracles, and virtue to be released in your life. As you go to the hospital, to your home, to your job, believe that the miracles of God will be released through you.

DECLARATIONS TO RELEASE THE GIFT OF HEALING

I pray that God would anoint me to have virtue in my life—not only in my hands but also in my clothes so that wherever I go and encounter sick people, they will be healed when I touch them.

Heavenly Father, I receive an anointing for healing in my hands and in my body. Let virtue be released through me and through my clothing. Let Your power be released through me so that wherever I go people will be healed.

Heavenly Father, as I fast and pray, increase Your healing virtue in my body and in my clothing, that wherever I go and whoever I touch will be healed.

I believe for miracles to flow through my life in Jesus's name.

SUBMITTING YOURSELF TO GOD'S SERVICE

The people are crying for You, Lord. Anoint me like You did Benjamin, and send me to this land as a spiritual captain over Your people, that they might be saved out of the hand of the enemy (1 Sam. 9:16).

You have anointed me and delivered me from the hands of my enemies, just as You did for King David (2 Sam. 12:7).

I will arise and be cleansed, I will be clothed by the Holy Spirit and be anointed as I worship in Your house, and I will eat of the bread of life from the table that You have set before me (2 Sam. 12:20).

Turn Your face toward me, O God, and remember Your mercy toward me as one You have anointed (2 Chron. 6:42).

In Your love for righteousness and hatred of wickedness, You have anointed me with the oil of gladness more than all those around me (Ps. 45:7; Heb. 1:9).

You have anointed me with fresh oil, and now I am strong as a wild ox (Ps. 92:10).

Turn Your face toward me, Your anointed (Ps. 132:10).

My burden shall be taken away from off my shoulder, and the yoke removed from off my neck and destroyed, because of the anointing upon my life (Isa. 10:27).

PRAYERS FOR PERSONAL ANOINTING

Just as the Lord gave a specific anointing to Aaron, so too, by reason of the anointing, I have been given a specific ministry gift to use, which shall be mine—and my children's—by God's ordinance forever (Num. 18:8).

I know that the Lord saves His anointed, and He will hear me when I call and will come to my aid with the saving strength of His right hand (Ps. 20:6).

God has prepared a table before me in the presence of mine enemies: He has anointed my head with oil; my cup runneth over (Ps. 23:5).

The Lord is my strength, and, as His anointed, I will be saved by His strength (Ps. 28:8).

Just like the blind man whom Jesus told to wash in the pool of Siloam, I will demand that God's anointing power will flow through His servants today and touch my eyes, so that I may wash and receive spiritual sight (John 9:11).

I will sing of the mercies of the Lord forever; with my mouth will I make known His faithfulness to all generations, that all will seek after Him for themselves (Ps. 89:1).

I will praise thy wonders, O Lord, and tell of Your faithfulness also in the congregation of the saints (Ps. 89:5).

Lord, keep Your eyes upon Your faithful servants in this land, that we may dwell with You, and help us to walk in a perfect way so that we may serve You and cause many to seek Your anointing also (Ps. 101:6).

Father, make me like Stephen—full of faith and power—that I may do great wonders and miracles among the people (Acts 6:8).

I will stay full of the Holy Ghost and of faith so that many will say, "He was a good man," and because of Your anointing on my life many people will be added unto the Lord (Acts 11:24).

I have been anointed to open their eyes and to turn them from darkness to light, and from the power of Satan unto God, that they may receive forgiveness of sins and inheritance among those who are sanctified by faith that is in me (Acts 26:18).

I thank my God through Jesus Christ for all my anointed leaders, whose faith is spoken of throughout the whole world (Rom. 1:8). May I become like them.

I will allow the power of God's anointing to bring a harvest of the fruit of the Spirit—His love, joy, peace, longsuffering, gentleness, goodness, faith, meekness, and temperance—that draws others to demand His anointing for themselves (Gal. 5:22–23).

I thank Christ Jesus our Lord, who has enabled me, for counting me faithful and putting me into the ministry (1 Tim. 1:12).

I work miracles according to the hearing of faith and not by the works of the law (Gal. 3:5).

God has called me, and He is faithful to do through me that for which I was called (1 Thess. 5:24).

I will receive strength to conceive that seed of the dreams, anointing, and gifts that God has placed in me. I declare in faith that those same dreams, anointing, and gifts will be delivered, because God, who has promised, has declared me faithful (Heb. 11:11).

The anointing of God abides in me and teaches me all things. The anointing reveals the truth to me as I abide in God (1 John 2:27).

I offer excellent sacrifices before You, O God, because You have counted me righteous by my faith. Testify of the gifts You have anointed me with, that even after I am dead my eternal works will speak (Heb. 11:4).

I decree and declare that I will obey God and, by faith, go to where He has called me so I may receive my inheritance (Heb. 11:8).

PRAYERS THAT RELEASE GENERATIONAL ANOINTING

Just as You anointed Aaron and his sons after him, so You have anointed and consecrated my children and me to Your service (Exod. 29:29).

I believe that I have been anointed by God just as He anointed my father, that I may minister unto God in my ministry gifting and that my family may be an everlasting priesthood throughout all our generations (Exod. 40:15).

You have raised me up a faithful priest, and I will do according to what is in Your heart and mind for me to do. You have built a secure house for my family and me, and we will be Your anointed servants forever (1 Sam. 2:35).

You are my tower of salvation, O Lord, and You have shown mercy to me, Your anointed, and to my children for generations to come (2 Sam. 22:51).

Because of Your anointing on my life, You have granted all the future generations of my family and me great deliverance and mercy (Ps. 18:50).

I believe God and take His warnings to heart; therefore, He will shelter my family, and we will all be saved. By faith, we are heirs of His righteousness (Heb. 11:7).

I offer to God my children and declare them His, and in faith I receive the promises of God (Heb. 11:17).

I release blessing upon my children. I have faith in what God is going to do for them in the future (Heb. 11:20).

I will continually speak blessing over my future generations and will worship God, even in my old age (Heb. 11:21).

I cover all of my firstborn—children, dreams, the fruit of my labor—with the blood of Jesus, and the angel of death will not touch them but will pass over (Heb. 11:28).

PRAYERS THAT ACTIVATE YOUR HEALING ANOINTING

I thank You, God, that You have heard my prayers and have released healing to Your people (2 Chron. 30:20).

The Spirit of the Lord God is upon me because the Lord has anointed me to preach good tidings to the poor. He has sent me to heal the brokenhearted; to comfort all who mourn; to give them beauty for ashes, the oil of joy for mourning, and the garment of praise for the spirit of heaviness, that they may be called trees of righteousness, the planting of the Lord, that He may be glorified (Isa. 61:1–3).

O God, You will bring health and healing. You will heal the people and reveal to them the abundance of peace and truth (Jer. 33:6).

I quicken the people of God to fear the Lord, so that the Sun of Righteousness may arise with healing in His wings (Mal. 4:2).

Just like Jesus, I am released to go and preach the gospel of the kingdom and to heal all kinds of sickness and diseases so that the name and fame of Jesus goes throughout the whole world (Matt. 4:23).

Let it be that sick people who are afflicted with various diseases and torments and those who are demon possessed, epileptics, and paralytics come my way that I may heal them in the name of Jesus (Matt. 4:24).

I accept the call: I will go and heal those who need healing (Matt. 8:7).

I am moved with compassion for the sick because they are weary and scattered, like sheep having no shepherd (Matt. 9:36).

I will heal the sick, cleanse the lepers, raise the dead, and cast out demons. As freely as I have received, I will freely give (Matt. 10:8).

I declare that the power of the Lord is present to heal His people (Luke 5:17).

I receive the multitudes. I will speak to them about the kingdom of God and will heal them in the name of Jesus (Luke 9:11).

I will stretch out my hand to heal so that signs and wonders may be done through the name of Jesus (Acts 4:30).

By the word of the Lord, the people are healed (Ps. 107:20).

I will be a faithful ambassador who brings health and healing (Prov. 13:17).

As the sick are laid at my feet, I declare that the healing anointing of Jesus will flow through me, and they will be healed (Matt. 15:30).

I will lay hands on the sick so that they may be healed, and they will live (Mark 5:23).

I rebuke unclean spirits and sickness in children. By the anointing of Jesus Christ, I will heal them and return them to the care of their parents (Luke 9:42).

I may not have silver; I may not have gold, but what I do have is the anointing to heal those who are sick. In the name of Jesus Christ of Nazareth, I speak to those who are ill: "Rise up and walk" (Acts 3:6–7).

I will observe intently and see that those who come have the faith to be healed. I will call them out of their infirmity, saying, "Stand straight on your feet!" And they will leap and walk (Acts 14:9–10).

I will go in to visit the sick and pray with them. I will lay my hands on them and heal them (Acts 28:8).

As the sick are brought before me, I am able, by Your anointing, to heal them because of their faith. I declare to them, "Be of good cheer; your sins have been forgiven" (Matt. 9:2).

I declare that by my great faith, it will be to me as I desire. My children are made whole—body, mind, and spirit—this very hour (Matt. 15:28).

I can see the faith of Your people, God. I speak healing and forgiveness over them (Mark 2:5).

Let it be that those whom I touch will be made well, healed from their infirmity, and set free to live in peace (Mark 5:34).

I walk in the anointing of Jesus Christ, healing people and giving sight to the blind according to their faith in God (Mark 10:52).

I am filled with the Holy Spirit and with power to do good, healing all who are oppressed by the devil, and I know that God is with me just as He was with Jesus (Acts 10:38).

I declare that my faith-filled prayers will deliver the sick and the Lord will raise them up. Their sins will be forgiven (James 5:15).

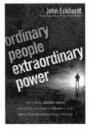
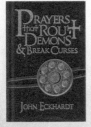

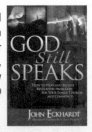